SO YOU'RE THE ONE
SOME OF MY SUSAN STORIES

KEVIN M. ST.ONGE

Dedication

These pages are dedicated to the four women for whom I had the honor and privilege to prepare and deliver eulogies or remembrances.

The first was my sister, Sandy Ann St.Onge in 1995. I co-wrote, then delivered, "A Letter From Mom" during her funeral mass.

Next were my Grandmothers, Jeanne St.Onge (Memere) in 2001 and Adrienne Baillargeon (Grandmaman) in 2004. Gratitude and chocolate chip cookies were the respective themes for those remarks.

Then, Susan Dalton St.Onge in 2018. These stories are an extension of the words shared during her Celebration of Life.

All four women have inspired me, and countless others, in too many ways to know.

I hope our Spirits connect again in our next lifetimes.

Contents

Prologue

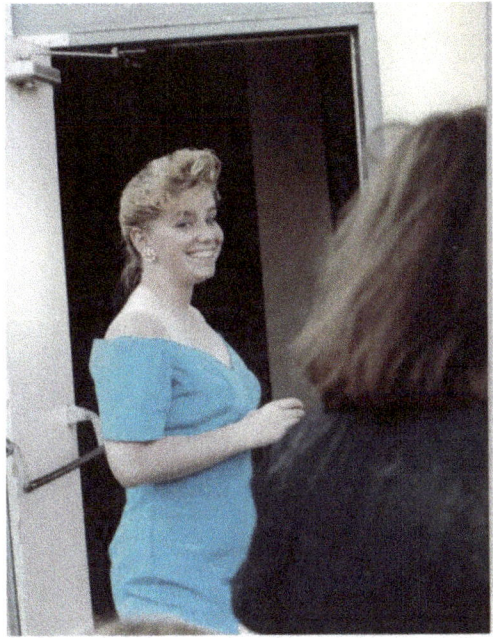

May 17, 1991
Townhouse C-1
Marist College
Poughkeepsie, New York

Senior year. Finals were done. Graduation was right around the corner but the Senior Formal was that night. I remember the date, May 17, not only because it is my Dad's birthday but because in 1991 it became a signature moment in my life.

I did not have a girlfriend at the time. I was taking a freshman to the dance because we were friendly, she lived close by and she wanted to go. It would be fun! It was early afternoon and my roommate and I had just gotten back from picking up flowers for our dates and were hanging out in the common area of our 13-student townhouse. Most of our housemates were scattered around campus enjoying the last bits of collegiate fun.

In walks this beautiful blonde 21-year-old woman. Flowing flowery blouse, a pair of clear plastic-rimmed Oakleys holding her hair back and the bluest eyes anyone has ever seen—she had late spring in New York written all over her.

Her smile, seemingly permanently affixed to her face, started with a twinkle in her eyes and spread from here-to-there.

"Hi. I'm Susan Dalton," she said to me, reaching out a hand.

Startled by how stunningly beautiful she was and with zero game in my repertoire (then or now), my response was prophetic: "so you're the one."

Chapter 1
The End, Almost

A Celebration of God's Beautiful Creation
Susan Dalton St.Onge
June 30, 2018, 11:15 AM
St. Helen's Church

Entrance	*"Fight Song"*
Opening Blessing	Father Michael Saporito
Video Presentation	Susan's Heritage and Baby Susan
	Faces of Susan
	Susan Loves Kevin
	Susan Loves her Children
Musical Interlude	*"When I Was Your Man"*
	"Heart and Soul"
Susan's story	Kevin St.Onge
Closing Prayer	Father Michael Saporito
Recessional	*"Maybe"*

* All songs performed by Nora J. St.Onge, accompanied by Mary Lu Farrell

Her temporary urn was a pleasant white wooden box. It had an embroidered ribbon around it with little pink roses and gilded edges. Tasteful. She would have liked it. It was provided by the funeral home and was placed reverently on the center of the Altar.

Standing next to it, near the spot where we married just shy of 24 years earlier, where our eldest daughter Molly was baptized, I called our 14-year-old daughter Nora to the front of the congregation to be recognized for singing at her Mother's Celebration of Life.

It was surreal.

That Nora had the fortitude, much less the talent, to sing the songs she did, "Fight Song", "When I Was Your Man", and "Heart and Soul", was gut wrenching. How was I possibly going to follow her and keep it together long enough to tell Susan's story to the approximately 300 family members and friends collectively grieving our loss?

Knowing this would be near impossible, I am so grateful I planned ahead—and stalled.

I asked 16-year-old Molly and 8-year-old Ella to join us to share the spot where Mommy and I were married on October 1, 1994. As they stood there, front and center, I slowly backed away to the podium and began calling people to join them on the Altar:

Sue Letwink, Amanda Hosmer, Annalisa Dalton, Denise Ferbas, Alisa Wasserman, Booma, Grammy, Rebecca, Lori Fitzgerald, Terrine Joe, Alexis Calabrese... I continued to call local women Susan knew through the girls, Wilkes College women, women from Susan's professional life at Stevens Institute of Technology, Princeton University, the local JCC, indeed all the women present who called Susan a friend or were touched by her in any way.

I asked them all to "... assemble around her daughters ..."

It was an impressive sight. Dozens of women of all ages standing on God's Altar. I don't know if the men in the pews or Father Michael Saporito knew what to make of this. But, I know what my words were to those in attendance.

Molly, Nora, Ella—you are surrounded by a formidable force. Please join hands—this is an unbreakable chain of Love forged in the fire of sisterhood. Susan's Sisterhood.

Your Mother shared her Spirit, in one way or another, with all these women. And they shared theirs with her.

They know Mommy and therefore they know you. Mommy and I are asking them to watch over you, in practical every day terms and in Spiritual and emotional terms and in ways that I just won't be able to do as your Father.

She trusted them with her love and compassion and we are calling on them to reflect her dignity, grace, fierce love for the underdog and all that was good about her, back on you.

I am asking that each of them pledge to keep track of you through the years, help us celebrate your milestones and accomplishments, take you to Ladies Nights out (when appropriate), or simply take you for coffee and be a presence in your lives as a constant reminder of the woman your Mother was.

Thank you.

Next, my turn, on the Altar.

Alone.

I began.

After kicking cancer into remission in 2015, Susan was set to speak at a small gathering of people about her experience so we prepared the following statement for her to deliver:

Cancer changes your life forever. However, I consider myself blessed in so many ways.

Early detection is the key. Information is power.

And we are so fortunate to live in this time, and in this place, where medical technology gives us a <u>chance</u> to survive.....

And, survive is what I intend to do.

With 3 children—4, if you count my husband Kevin—I have obligations and unfinished works.

This past year was an ordeal but it made me stronger, physically, mentally and spiritually.

So thank you for your continued contributions and support for all cancer-related causes. With your help we will find a cure and preventative measures.

Again, thank you!

With love and kindness (and encouragement to you to go have a beer) I am,

Susan Dalton St.Onge

Quintessential Susan. Optimistic in the face of adversity. Ever concerned about the welfare of others, particularly as it related to having a beer (she was of Irish descent after all!), she had every intention of surviving.

But, as the old saying goes, "People plan, God laughs."

Chapter 2
The Early Years: 1991-1994(ish)

I felt conflicted telling Susan's story that day. She was born to a family who loved her. She made many friends throughout her life who loved her. But, she chose to love me. It was her conscious decision to exclude others from the kind of love she chose to share with me. My conflict, therefore, was whether to tell her story or tell our story.

I knew mine was only one of many perspectives of her life. As selfishly as I wanted to keep the moment between me and her, I knew full well that there were many people in attendance that day who knew Susan differently than I did. Even now, I grudgingly respect that. It represents the fullness of a life well-lived that a person might relate and be relatable to a diversity of people.

As "the husband," I felt it was my obligation to retell our story (which I did). However, I also wanted to weave in other threads from the rich tapestry of her life so that all in attendance would feel included, as the significant players in her life that they were, and as she would have wanted. I am not sure if I accomplished that then or here in these pages. I will share some of those stories later in this book, but, on that day, I started at our beginning.

My Life with Susan - we were married October 1, 1994 on this spot.

Susan was a Peer Minister here at St. Helen's in the 80's where she met Tom Hanna who later introduced us. All of our girls have grown up here. Some were baptized here, Molly and Nora were Altar Servers. Nora has sung in the choir. Ella received her First Communion and Molly made her Confirmation here this Spring.

We are so blessed to be able to Celebrate Susan here in God's Home—a place where so many blessings in our lives have occurred. Thank you Father Michael.

So, this is how we will celebrate Susan—today and in days and years to come - with stories of her . . . you saw the pictures in the slide shows—all the smiles and all the laughter and all the good times. I would like to share some of the small part I played in her life's story. . .

<u>Friday, May 17, 1991 - Smitten at Marist College</u>

Anyone who knew me in the early years knew that I was what is politely referred to as a "late bloomer." So late, in fact, that we are still waiting. Anyway, I managed to get through high school and college without a serious relationship. The girls, now women, of Milford Area Senior High School and Marist College apparently didn't see whatever Susan would see, eventually. There were a few short-term girlfriends but nothing stuck. Therefore, as college was winding down and the big formal was coming up, I was a prime target for a freshman who just wanted to go to the Senior Formal.

My housemate, Tom Hanna, was from Westfield, New Jersey. If memory serves, his girlfriend dumped him second semester, senior year, so he was also a free agent. 1991 was around the time of Major League Baseball and the National Football League strikes and lockouts so there was a lot of talk of "replacement players." Tom and I both referred to our dates as "replacement players."

Poughkeepsie, New York, is only about an hour and a half north of Westfield, New Jersey. Tom opted to dip his toe into the old high school dating pool and asked a high school classmate to the Formal. Tom and Susan knew each other from serving as Peer Ministers at St. Helen's Parish and, of course, high school. Tom played soccer, Susan played saxophone in the marching band.

I don't think they dated in high school, but Susan was wrapping up at Wilkes College (now University) and didn't have any other attachments. She was always open to try something that sounded fun so she said yes to the 95 mile drive to Poughkeepsie.

Suffice to say, love conquers all. Neither of us disrespected our respective dates but there was no question that from her first, "Hi. I'm Susan Dalton," to my "so you're the one…" our energies connected. We spent that entire afternoon and evening at the Formal looking for excuses to bump into each other and exchange pleasantries. I don't remember all the details of that night but I do remember that I had never been so smitten. And, weirdly for me, it felt like she was too.

The basis for my "so you're the one" comment is important to our story. Susan had recently had breast reduction surgery. Tom, of course, told all us guys in the C-1 Townhouse about how his date had a "reduction." Being 22-year-old knuckleheads, we were all as impressed as 15-year-old boys. As such, as Susan and I started dating, much mystery surrounded my comment. Was I saying that "you're the one who will fall in love with me and be mine forever?" Sort of like when Bobby kissed Millicent in the *Brady Bunch* and saw fireworks. Or, was I referring to the fact that "she was the one who had a breast reduction?" (Insert giggle of 15-year-old boy here). Whatever may or may not have been in my mind then, anyone who reads this entire book will know the truth of the matter.

Equally important to our story is that, with very few exceptions, Susan was an open book. Things like privacy and HIPAA meant little to her. A solid confidant, she would never breach anyone else's confidentiality, but she was always very open about her own "stuff." I will try to honor and respect that in these pages while maintaining her dignity and grace. She was fully transparent regarding her own breast reduction. Done for health reasons, lower back pain, etc., she nonetheless laughed at jokes about well-endowed women. Her college nickname, after all, was "Double D Dalton."

*The C-1 Townhouse Guys—my friends to this day
(L-R) Me (with hair), Terry Hosmer, Steve Hoffmann,
Tom Hanna, James Joseph, Anthony Azzara*

One of her college friends went on to become a professional comedian. He did/does a riff about the female thought process behind getting a breast reduction compared to the male thought process. The riff goes that women contend that it is always based on health reasons, which Susan clearly related to. The male thought process, as you might expect, can be summed up in three words according to Dave Russo, "suck it up."

Susan did not agree with it but she loved it!

Susan Dalton and Tom Hanna
Marist College Senior Formal
May 17, 1991

Summer, 1991

Fast-forward a couple weeks and I was back in Southern New Hampshire and Susan was back in Westfield, New Jersey. We might as well have been worlds apart! She was working at home that summer and heading back to Wilkes for one more semester (that is a whole other story!). I was getting ready to head to Washington, D.C., to attend law school at Catholic University.

I knew (because she told me) that she was not seeing Tom. They were friends. So I took a chance and <u>typed</u> a letter to mail to her. Yes, U.S. Postal Service, regular mail!

The letter was suggestive, probably ridiculous, but hopefully endearing. (Reading it today gives me "dumb chills," but it worked in its time!)

Tuesday June 25, 1991

Dear Sue:

Hey bud, long time no see . . . like we're old friends from the neighborhood or something right?!!! How's Hanna's "woman" doing this summer? He get you to the beach yet? Volleyball and all that stuff?

The way you were moving on the dance floor at the formal you must be o.k. in the sand! (Now, now, that was not suggestive or anything -- not as suggestive as the way you dance anyway . . .)

Yes, even in letters, we Marist people can be rude, crude and obnoxious -- I swear, I wasn't like that before I met Tom!

Seriously, how's your summer going? I heard from Hanna-time -- he's busy with the "Game" as always. Camps and the beach, must be nice. . .

Are you among the ranks of unemployed. Refresh my memory, did you finish school or do you still have some time to put in?

Hope you had a good time at Marist last month -- can you believe it's been a month? Man, time flies doesn't it? I know Laura and some of the girls liked you alot. It was cool the way everybody seemed to hit-it off right away. The C-1 guys are not known for their hospitality but I thought we had some fun . . .

So what's the deal, are we gonna see you at the Jersey Shore when the New Hampshire kid takes his volleyball show on the road? Forget the Pro-beach Tour -- the kid from that cow state is coming down to show you how the game is played...

Looks like some of us are making the trek down to Belmar or something in the middle of July, it'd be great to see you if you can make it with Hanna. Let me know what the calendar looks like -- we were thinking the second or third week. . .

Hope you like the picture, unlike most people, you both have natural smiles . . .

Hope to see you in the Sand,

Kevin

P.S. You have to put in touch with you friend at Catholic U.

I sent it wondering if she would respond. She did! Her letter was also suggestive, funny and most definitely endearing. We could feel each other's energy even in written letters.

July 1, 1991

Kevin,

Hi there! How are you? Well you blew me away! What a letter — you Marist people! I don't have anything to type on so you'll have to deal with this scribble!

I had such an awesome time at Marist. Everyone was so much fun! If you talk to Laura, tell here I said "Hello." She's a sweetheart! You guys are absolutely crazy! Compared to some of the other schools that I've partied at, I must say Marist was the best experience — yet — haha!

I'm at school right now, I have to take one class to

graduate in August and let
me say it's no fun! Here I am
"among the ranks of the unemployed"
but otherwise at home I work
for my father. I had my second
test today, I got a 93 on my
first test, not too shabby. My
paper is due this friday + the final is
next friday. But I have been hitting
the shore mostly every weekend.
I haven't really talked to Hanna
that much; he's probably busy
with - what else - volley ball.
        Hey if that New Hampshire
kid is taking his circuit to
the Jersey Shore, I don't know,
I'll have to think about it! Well
if you're going to be in Belmar
I think I can make the long
journey to the shore! I've
got to check out how you

move in the sand — not to be
suggestive — ha! I'll definately
be able to check out the
action. My calendar looks good.
Thanks for the picture, it's
a good shot. You'll have to
get in touch with me when
you arrive in Jersey, we'll hit
the bars, and then maybe the
sand!
Hope to see you soon —
Love
Susan

We secretly stole time on the land-line telephones at our parents'
homes (occasionally being scolded for incurring long-distance
charges!) and continued to write letters. No cell phones, no texting
or even email! We learned about each other through those letters and
abbreviated toll calls.

More importantly, we arranged that we would both be invited to
a party at Tom's house in New Jersey (yes that Tom!) in August
when I would be driving to Washington. Two and one-half months
after meeting ever so briefly, and then writing letters, we would see
each other again! It seemed like an eternity. We could not wait! She
was cool about it. Not me! I was giddy with anticipation!

(After she passed, I found she had a couple of shoe boxes filled
with our letters. Her boxes looked just like the ones I had!
Interestingly, I found that she had volumes of her writings that pre-

dated me! Truthfully, it was hard to read some of those Sue-notes to other boys. She also had a whole collection of notes she clearly had passed to her girlfriends in class at school. Tiny little folded pieces of paper with random ramblings clearly important to her 13-18 year old self!)

August 17, 1991 – Summer Party – The First Kiss

I don't remember anything about the party except that I was sleeping at Tom's house before getting up early the next morning to drive the rest of the way to D.C. Oh, and that Susan and I became inseparable. Once we started talking that night, it continued for 27 years!

We spoke over the keg, filling red Solo cups for others. We moved far away from the speakers blaring late '80s and very early '90s music so we wouldn't miss a single word the other was saying. She told me about her summer and plans to return to Wilkes for one more semester. I told her about going to law school and what I wanted to do with my life. I joked that I hoped to marry a lawyer and be a stay-at-home dad and coach Little League.

We were kids. 22 years old. In shape—her from 4 years of college soccer (she was a freshman on the first women's soccer team at Wilkes in 1987, a connection she remained proud of in her adult life)—me from helping my Dad build a stone wall back home in Milford, New Hampshire, among other activities.

Eventually the evening led to her sitting on her early '80s light blue Toyota Camry in front of Tom's house on Norwood Drive in Westfield.

I always remembered the name of the street, Norwood, because we were not far removed from the New York Giants (Susan had a Mark Bavaro #89 game shirt) beating the Buffalo Bills in the 1991 Super Bowl. The Bills' placekicker Scott Norwood missed a 47-yard field goal attempt in the final seconds of Super Bowl XXV on January 27, 1991. Susan, her brother Chris and band-wagon fan father, John, of course loved that the Giants won. They also took a little too much pleasure rubbing it in years later when the Giants denied my New England Patriots an undefeated season in 2007. In that Super Bowl, the football defied physics, actually sticking to the face mask of receiver David Tyree's helmet like velcro. Or, illegal stickum? The "helmet catch," as it would later be known, never should have happened. The play should have been whistled dead earlier because quarterback Eli Manning was "in the grasp." But, again, I digress.

Back to that summer evening in 1991. It had to be 1 or 2 AM and the street light cast just enough glow to see a hint of her blue eyes and the occasional sparkles that emerge from a woman's skin, the ones that look like mini stars. What is that anyway? I mean, who puts glitter on their face? Is that natural? Her blonde hair, almost bleached from her summer weekends on the beach in Manasquan, New Jersey, framed her face and fell to below her shoulders. Tame-ish at that moment, I would later learn that she could tease it out to look like she was Bon Jovi's little sister.

She was goofing on me for wanting to be a lawyer. I didn't mind, I was lost in her presence and still could not believe she was talking to me. Her undoing, or maybe it was her plan all along (a point debated for years after), was the following exchange:

Her: "How can you tell when a lawyer is lying?"

Still in the trance of her beauty, I stammered eloquently: "Um, uh, I don't know?"

Her: "His lips are moving..." as she proceeded to giggle at her joke.

Snapped out of my dreamlike-state, and without missing a beat, I responded:

"Would these lips be lying if they did this...?"

I planted one on her. It was a real kiss, with a real girl, under the real moon!

We both took credit—she said she set me up, I said I was just that good. I think, over time, we came to realize that we were both right.

During that time, she sent me a picture of her from senior year of high school leaning against that '80s light blue Toyota Camry. Light blue eye-liner matched the car and her Flock of Seagulls inspired hair (you have to be from the '80s to understand that reference), mixed with her killer smile was more than I could stand. The original photo was slightly blurry. This digital version captured it as is. Framed and on my desks all through law school, I fell in love with Susan Dalton from that kiss and that photo.

Chapter 3
Law School Hijinks,
Trips to Wilkes and Yankee Stadium

After the summer party, I continued on my way to Washington, D.C., to start law school. Getting up early that first morning to leave Westfield, I decided to call Susan at her house at around 8:00 AM. Her parents were away, so I figured that would be fine. I wasn't counting on her older brother Chris answering the phone. He was understandably frustrated at a phone call at that hour. Regardless, Susan got on the phone and invited herself to visit me at school.

My dorm at Catholic University was called Gibbons Hall. It was located right in front of the Basilica of the National Shrine of the Immaculate Conception. No, that was not prophetic! Susan came to visit me at school after I had been there for a couple of weeks. It was amazing to see her. It was amazing to have somebody to tour with around Washington.

I introduced her to my law school classmates and she immediately hit it off with Marybeth Duda, John Sinisko, Joe Haggerty, Michael Hagerty (no relation to Joe!) Walter Galas, Lisa Mele (who later became Mrs. Walter Galas!), Dave Rivera and Jennifer Ulwick. In very short order, my crew became her crew: the start of a pattern whereby anybody I was friends with immediately gravitated to Susan and became her friend. For the rest of our lives together, Susan won over my friends and they would gang up on me!

Marybeth was fascinating. She and Susan bonded immediately. So much so that early on, Susan told me that if we weren't dating, she would expect me to be with Marybeth! That never happened. Years later Susan and I attended Marybeth's untimely funeral when she died in an ATV accident in Connecticut.

We continued to write letters (filling up our respective shoe boxes!) and, sporadically, spoke on the telephone (long distance toll charges were expensive, especially when we had to pay them ourselves!).

She went back to Wilkes College for her final semester and invited me to visit her there. Jumping at the chance to drive the 225 miles to Wilkes from D.C., I couldn't wait to get away from my dorm, and more importantly, to spend time with her. On campus, she showed me her apartment, where she was working as a manager for the wrestling team and where she played soccer.

She introduced me to some of her friends but there weren't many there that semester. Most of her class had graduated the spring before, but she had to complete another semester to make up for an abbreviated first semester freshman year. Her roommate that first year had significant personal issues, leaving school very abruptly without any notice. Susan was a very empathic person and that roommate incident impacted her, causing her to withdraw from school that semester.

The silver lining to that story is that her roommate that first semester wound up living in our neighborhood in Fanwood, New Jersey! The woman's son was in our daughter's kindergarten class. So, twenty-plus years after an abrupt farewell, Susan reconnected with her roommate and they resumed a friendship that included running road races and baking birthday cakes for our kids!

Those kinds of "small world" experiences occurred regularly in Susan's life and she reveled in them. Although none were quite as dramatic as that one.

Anyway, back to my first visit to Wilkes. She was so happy to take me to a Wilkes-Barre landmark called the Chicken Coop for the best wings and beer around. Anybody from that part of Pennsylvania would know the Chicken Coop. For years following, whenever we were in the area, we had to stop for wings and beer.

The first time I visited her I remember not wanting to leave. Dreading leaving, we had the first of a lifetime of long goodbyes. As a woman of Irish descent, she could never simply say "so long" and walk away. That too was prophetic.

Her "closing conversations" were always interminably long with everyone! The long goodbye was not simply a parallel to her long illness and passing, but it represented her in everyday life, unable to end conversations to avoid offending whoever she was speaking with. She was not alone in this habit: the worst offenders are several family members who will remain nameless.

Where was I? Oh yeah, my first departure from Wilkes. Of course we kissed, and no, the lips still were not lying! When I finally got in the car, she leaned in through the rolled-down window. I was thinking (hoping) it was for another kiss, but it was actually to put in a cassette tape (yes, that was the way we listened to music back then). Her plan was to hit play and then watch me drive-away. I screwed that up by sitting there and listening to the song which made things sort of awkward.

Ever mindful of being polite, she held her tongue and tried not to tell me to drive away. Eventually, I did. The song was Harry Connick Jr.'s "Recipe for Love". It had its intended impact as evidenced by the letter I wrote to her later that month.

The trials and tests of character I referred to in the letter were in response to the story she shared with me about freshman year of college and challenges she faced while earning her degree in early childhood education. She had a bad experience during her student-teaching stint and it rocked her confidence. So much so, when she completed her degree at Wilkes, she had no interest in teaching children.

3:45 A.M.   9/28/91

Susan,

You're probably all snug in your bed at home – off in Dalton Dreamland – sweet dreams I hope – Nothing but the best for the best.. The comfort of your own pillow on which to rest your head, the assurance that when the sun comes up in a few hours, you know where you are – and where you're going... I envy you Sue Dalton, despite all your recent trials and tests of character, you at least outwardly project a confident determined woman. Determined to find happiness with every smile, you seem content to accept people for what they are, and you leave it at that.

It's truly remarkable that we've just met (sort of) because when we're together, I feel as if we've been together for a lifetime. I can only hope you feel a tenth of the attraction to me that I have felt for you... Each time the phone rings, it has to be Sue, anyone else on the other end is a disappointment. (except for Mom!) Every pause during the day is a reflection of or on a moment spent with you.

Why am I writing at this time of day? Well my last waking thoughts each day are of you... so before my head rests on my pillow I wanted to share my day-ending thoughts with the person who brings a smile to my face, just because she's smiling too – A guy named Sue

She would eventually regain her mojo as a Mother. And, her last job before she passed was working as a teacher's aide in a pre-kindergarten program at our local Jewish Community Center in Scotch Plains, New Jersey (JCC, think YMCA in other parts of the country). But, in the Fall of 1991, after four years of believing she would go on to a teaching career and all that entailed, she was decisive in walking away from it. The details are not relevant now, but parents and administrators can be extremely cruel to teachers, especially new ones and those who are training.

Wilkes College, 1991
Susan, John and Ann Dalton

Looking back on it now, I am so proud of her for coming full circle from that experience and returning to a pre-K program. She loved working with the littles, as she called them! She had so much joy being with young, innocent and impressionable children. As a high-vibration person herself, she resonated with them. She felt so comforted in the presence of littles—and, although she wasn't Jewish, they loved her at the JCC. So much so, they planted a tree on the campus in her honor.

The Alarm Clock Incident

Those three years in Washington were a blast. We would get together every second or third weekend, either in Wilkes-Barre, at her home in Westfield, or the family beach house in Manasquan, New Jersey. She would often take the train to Washington to visit me. She caused quite a stir one return trip when the doors to the metro liner failed to open at her stop in Metropark (she was in the wrong car to get off) and she saw her Father on the platform as she continued on to New York City well after midnight! She was always of such good cheer. Even that couldn't dampen her enthusiasm to travel to see me, but, after that, she preferred to drive herself.

Susan also loved my law school friends and housemates. She joked around with them and learned that at least one of them was more than ready for her antics. Joe Haggerty, one of my housemates from Scranton, Pennsylvania, which is very close to Wilkes Barre, and Susan used to bust each others', er, balls, over all things regarding Central Pennsylvania. It was mostly local humor that the rest of us simply didn't understand (or care to!).

One night, while Joe was out of the house, Susan decided to set his alarm clock for 3:00 AM (this was before cell phones so we had such things as dedicated alarm clocks). The next morning, she had a great chuckle at Joe's expense because he looked very haggard. She called him "Haggard Haggerty" and thought she was so funny.

Not content to be out-done, Joe decided that next night, when he knew Susan and I were going to be out on the town drinking and having fun, he would set my alarm clock for about 2:30 AM. It went off, we had a good laugh at it, then went back to sleep. Thirty minutes later, there went alarm number two, only we couldn't find the damn alarm clock! He had put HIS clock under the heaviest piece of furniture in my room and it was near impossible to get to it to shut it off. UGG!

I thought, "great, you two Central Pennsylvania juvenile delinquents, I'm collateral damage caught in YOUR crossfire." Anybody who knows me knows I absolutely need my beauty sleep. Back to sleep we went, but wouldn't you know, 45 minutes later at "oh my God it's early" o'clock, there's a third alarm! And it wasn't even under furniture or in the room! It was buried in my closet! The next morning, bleary eyed, her tail between her legs, Susan readily conceded to Haggard Haggerty that he was the master and she never called him that again.

Santa Claus Cabbies, Bras and U2

To know Susan is to know that she loves to have all kinds of fun, not just with other people's alarm clocks.

Thinking of her impromptu smile reminds me of a picture we have. I don't know who took it, but she was in New York City with some friends around the holidays and a taxi cab driver happened to be wearing a Santa Claus suit and beard. She thought that was the coolest thing and had to have her picture taken with the guy! Quintessential Susan.

In August, 1992, Susan, her brother Chris, his fiancé Annalisa and I drove from Manasquan, New Jersey, one weekend night to (Old) Yankee Stadium in the Bronx. Seventh row seats, left field along the runway stage for a U2 Zoo TV Tour concert. It was awesome! Packed house with the earthy aroma of marijuana (that some in our party may, or may not, have partaken in) mixed with the suggestion of sweaty summer bodies. The atmosphere was ripe for the unusual to happen.

Susan and Annalisa were having a great time, apparently talking about wanting to do something "different" when the band worked its way down the stage right next to us. Seventh row from the front, but when the band took to the runway, we were front row! Susan suggested they throw their bras on stage. Both women looked down at their respective chests, but, with Susan significantly more well-endowed, they decided Susan should throw hers.

Well, as I said, it was a hot and sticky summer night. Susan wore an old bra dating back to her breast reduction a couple of years earlier. As such, she really didn't mind throwing it on stage. Funny thing was, when Bono and the boys started working their way down the runway towards where we were standing, Susan, with her bra in her right hand over her head like the Statue of Liberty, froze when the band looked right at her. She didn't move!

In the next moment, however, we all saw her bra fluttering through the air then landing in a clump at Bono's feet. Here was the problem: the band saw that I was the one who threw it. With bemused looks on their faces, they just kept moving down the stage.

Susan and Annalisa were mortified! A roadie simply picked it up and tossed it onto a camera that was riding a rail up and down along the stage following the Irish boys. We watched that bra go back and forth all night and laughed harder and harder every time it came by.

I'm not sure what I proved that night, but Susan acknowledged that I was a man of, um, action!

Catholic University
Law School Graduation
1994

Chapter 4
Susan Says "Yes! Now Ask Me Again...!"

SUSAN EILEEN DALTON and KEVIN MICHAEL ST.ONGE

Susan Dalton is engaged to marry Kevin St. Onge

Mr. and Mrs. John J. Dalton of Westfield announce the engagement of their daughter, Susan Eileen, to Kevin Michael St.Onge, son of Mr. and Mrs. Richard St.Onge of Milford, N.H.

Ms. Dalton is a 1987 graduate of Westfield High School. She attended Wilkes University and received a bachelor's degree in psychology and education in 1991. She is employed at the firm of Bernstein & D'Arcangelo, P.C., in Summit.

Mr. St.Onge is a 1987 of Milford Area (N.H.) High School and graduated from Marist College in 1991 with a bachelor's degree in communications and political science. He currently is attending the Columbus School of law at Catholic University in Washington, D.C., and is employed by the law firm of George W. Campbell Jr. & Associates in Arlington, Va.

A wedding is planned for October 1994.

Following the U2/bra incident of 1992, I started my second year of law school. I knew then that I wanted to marry Susan. We talked about it and I would have married her right away but, ever sensible, she wanted me to graduate first.

During a visit to New Jersey in the Fall of 1992, I went for a bike ride while Susan's father, John, went for a run. This arrangement allowed me to do all the talking. Anybody who has met John knows it can be tough to get a word in edgewise at times. With what I had to say, and what I wanted to ask, all he had to say was yes.

Once he was sufficiently winded I told him that I loved his daughter and that, with his permission, I would like to marry her. Appropriately, gentlemanly, even for a Yankees/Giants fan, he said it was his daughter's decision and he would support whatever she decided. That was good enough for me!

Later that fall I skipped a weekend visit with Susan, instead driving to Syracuse, New York, to stay with a Marist College classmate and her family. Christy Bailey (DeRegis) put me up for a couple nights at her family's house while I spent the weekend with Mr. and Mrs. Renzo Munari. The Munari's daughter, Annalisa, was dating Susan's brother Chris.

(If the list of names and connections in these stories ever seems lengthy, that is how Susan often started conversations, "My high school friend's mother's best friend is my uncle's ex-girlfriend's hair dresser....")

Anyway, Annalisa was from the Syracuse area. Importantly, her father was a renaissance man. Among so many other talents and abilities, he was a gifted part-time jeweler.

He reminded me of my paternal grandfather, Edgar St.Onge. "Pepere" was a French Canadian carpenter. His workspace was filled with boxes marked with whatever their contents were, in French. Renzo's workshop felt very similar, dusty but organized, and his boxes were all marked in Italian!

That weekend, he and I designed Susan's engagement ring and I purchased his artisan services and the appropriate diamonds. I still remember it. The ring had one center stone with two trilliant cut stones on either side set in a gold band with six prongs.

I had the ring by Christmas 1992. It was killing me to hold onto it but I had to devise the perfect proposal. Although I had spent the holidays in New Hampshire, I went back to school during the intercession and managed to convince Susan to come visit me. By then, I was working part-time for a law firm in Arlington, Virginia. I concocted a story that we needed to drive to Richmond, Virginia, that weekend to attend a formal event by the Virginia Bar Association celebrating my employer, George W. Campbell, Jr., Esq.

It was a ruse of course. I called her boss in New Jersey (she was then working as a legal secretary) and covertly got her Monday off for a long weekend. I also made reservations for a bed-and-breakfast in Williamsburg, Virginia. Susan was to bring a little black dress for the event for George, but really it was for a formal dinner with me! Typical of Susan, she "forgot" to pack it, so before leaving D.C., we "had to go shopping." Sigh…

Driving south, the highway split, one direction toward Richmond and the other toward Williamsburg. When I veered to Williamsburg, she gave me a little sideways look, but, always up for an adventure, she was game!

We got to Williamsburg and immersed ourselves in the colonial period feel of the place. Susan knew I loved history. She was so good about honoring that interest throughout our life. She once gifted me a guided tour of the Gettysburg Battlefield—by horseback—for Father's Day.

Again, I'm getting ahead of the story!

That afternoon, we checked into our bed-and-breakfast. It was a nice room with a cannonball four-post bed and we dressed "formally" for dinner—we had reservations at the Williamsburg Inn.

It was my 24th birthday, January 16, 1993. Snow is not unheard of in central Virginia at that time of year, but it is rare. That evening, driving from the B&B to the restaurant, the snow began to fall. It was simply beautiful. It was simply meant to be.

The problem was, I didn't know where I was going to propose to her! That afternoon while we were tooling around Colonial Williamsburg, I was searching for a gazebo, a portico, anything that would have been appropriate for a proposal. I could not find anything suitable!

I finally decided to just do it right out there in the open of Duke of Gloucester Street, near the intersection with Palace Green Street, under an old colonial street lamp, across the cobblestone way from Bruton Parish Episcopal Church. Susan didn't understand why we were getting out of the car in the middle of a snowstorm in Colonial Williamsburg when we were supposed to be going to dinner.

Asking her to "...please humor me," we walked the 50 yards or so to the spot.

We were all dressed up. She had plenty of Aqua Net in her hair so when the snow landed on it, full flakes rested gently on her teased out curls. I tried to be eloquent but all I could manage to stammer, standing there, was, "I love you, I hope you love me forever...the best birthday present I could hope for is that you will be mine forever?"

I opened the ring box and she exclaimed, "No, no, no, you're not on your knee. You're doing it wrong!" So, in my suit pants, and with my long winter coat dragging in a puddle, I put one knee on the wet gravel sidewalk and, holding out the ring, I asked her again, "Will you marry me?"

Her hands butterflied in front of her face and she giggled like a school-girl saying, "ask me again, ask me again!" So, I asked her again. It seemed like an interminably long period of time with her standing there, a goofy smile, just fluttering her hands in front of her face. My knee was getting wet, and sore, and as I started to get up she finally shrieked "YES!" and snatched the ring from my fingers.

The rest of that night was a whirlwind! We found a payphone—yes, in Colonial Williamsburg, a payphone! She called her parents but they weren't home so she had to leave a message. I seem to recall Mrs. Dalton telling us later that when she heard the message she looked at Mr. Dalton and said, "He can't do that, he didn't talk to you," to which Mr. Dalton responded, "Yes he did." Susan called some of her girlfriends, including her very best girlfriend, Susan Letwink (now Howell).

I called home too but can't remember if I spoke with my family or left a message. Regardless, a few days later I received the following handwritten letter from my sister Sandy.

1/16/93   11:00 PM

Hey Kevin!

Congratulations bud! I'm so happy for you! After you called I knew what you were up to! :-)

I'm psyched to have a human being as a sister – Happy (our pet beagle who had recently passed away) was awesome but Sue is even better! :-)

I couldn't help but notice the way you related to each other over Christmas. You guys look like you were meant for each other.

Good luck to you bro!

Love,

Sandy

Years later, on subsequent trips to Williamsburg, with our "cannolial" girls (Molly and Nora couldn't say "colonial") it was imperative to Susan that we take pictures at the engagement spot with the kids.

The Engagement Spot with the Girls!

We enjoyed an amazing meal. We drank Riesling as if we knew what it was. She showed off her ring to those who were sitting around us. We were on cloud nine!

I had made arrangements with the innkeeper, a lovely woman whose name escapes me, to put a few engagement presents in the room, including a dozen roses (and a few things that I won't publish here!). They were waiting for Susan when we returned. That was when I told her that I had coordinated with her boss to give her Monday off. In classic Susan fashion, that was almost more exciting news to her than the engagement!

Ironically, on one of the return trips, years later with the kids, we went back to the bed-and-breakfast in search of that wonderful innkeeper. Sadly, we were told by her widower husband and then-adult daughter that she had since passed from breast cancer. Again, prophetic?

Chapter 5
We Say "I Do" - October 1, 1994

Graduating from law school in May 1994, I returned to New Hampshire to study for the bar exam and start a clerkship with the U.S. Magistrate Judge William H. Barry, Jr. I would be his last law clerk before he retired from the bench at the end of my year with him. Susan and I found a nice small house to rent in Concord but she did not come to live there until after the wedding.

At our rehearsal dinner in New Jersey, the night before the wedding, our families had us play "The Newlywed Game" by asking us questions to test how well we knew each other. One question we talked about for years later was, "Where will you live after the wedding?" With family in New Hampshire and New Jersey, without missing a beat, we simultaneously and diplomatically answered with a midpoint: "Connecticut!" I often wonder how different our lives might have been had we done exactly that.

Wedding day dawned as a rainy fall morning in Westfield, New Jersey. Nothing so inconsequential as the weather could dampen our enthusiasm for our day! About 150 people attended our church service at St. Helen's, the parish Susan grew up in. An Irish bagpiper added to the dewy atmosphere. We might as well have been in Dublin!

We were so happy to be sharing our special day with friends and family. Susan's Dad was there to walk her down the aisle. One of my college roommates, Anthony Azzara, sang. My dear friend from college and one of my law school housemates Joanne Prokopowicz (Sears) was a Eucharistic Minister and honored us by ministering Communion to us for the first time as husband and wife.

I wish I could remember all of the other family and friends who played a role in the wedding. Her brothers JT and Chris were groomsmen, together with my brother Matt and college classmates Steve Hoffmann and Terry Hosmer and law school classmate John Kacvinsky.

Susan's maid of honor was Susan Letwink (Howell). Her bridesmaids included my sister Sandy, sister-in-law Annalisa, her cousin Laura Shafer, and her girlfriends Laura McCord (Donnelly) and Alisa Tagliareni (Wasserman). If memory serves, Susan's Father and Aunt Jean Shafer did the readings.

When Monsignor James A. Burke rose to give his homily, it was an honor that he chose, instead, to share a letter I had written to Susan during our Pre-Cana exercises. He began: "I want to read a letter that Kevin wrote. I think it says so much more than I could say." The letter reads:

> *Love is all around.*
>
> *These words have inspired songs and poems. Today the emotion and the feeling of those words inspire me. While Susan and I are the ones getting married and committing the rest of our lives to*

each other, we know that we could not be in this position without the love that has been all around our lives from the very beginning

Our parents, our family, our friends, they are the ones who should take the credit, and some of the blame, for making us who we are.

We know and appreciate that our parents are in the minority of married couples. They are still married after over 25 years of marriage. They set a standard that Susan and I are committed to following, not merely in duration, but in the love that has gone into their marriages, their families and their lives.

Brothers and sisters can have the most confrontational relationships, however, following the fights and arguments there is maturity and mutual respect. With age comes understanding. It is hard to love a brother or sister when you are elbow-to-elbow in the backseat of a car on a long drive. Years later, however, it is impossible to imagine life any differently.

Friendships are reflections of our lives. Each friend we have somehow mirrors a part of life, either who we were, who we are or who we seek to become.

Love was all around. I felt it when Susan and I met because we were among friends.

Love was all around. I felt it when Susan took me home and when she came home with me because we were among family

Love is all around.

I feel it whenever we are together.

I can't describe it except to say that, like my family and friends, I can't imagine life without it.

Sincerely,

Kevin

In true Susan fashion, knowing the tech-guy wired me with a microphone for the wedding video, she leaned over during a pause in the proceedings to whisper into my chest that she "...wasn't wearing any underwear..."

I can't remember what her something borrowed was, but her something blue was having her bridesmaids write all over her leg in blue sharpie. Don't ask, I don't understand either.

Same spot the girls would later
be surrounded by "Susan's Sisterhood"

We had an absolute blast at our reception.

It started with a fun happy hour, then, per the custom of the day, when the guests were assembled in the dining room the wedding party was introduced. They entered through doors from the lobby area. Before we walked in, however, the doors were closed. All of our guests and wedding party were in the room waiting for us expectantly. It was our first moment together, alone, and in that moment we were giving our friends, and especially our families, a little gift.

We had arranged for a slideshow. It was set to music with pictures of Susan and I growing up separately and then coming together as a young couple. The coup de grâce was that the photographer was able to include a picture of us as a newly married couple using a fast developing slide film. He was able to insert that picture, taken a little over an hour before, as the last slide of the show. With the music trailing off and our first photo as husband and wife projected onto a big screen, Susan and I entered the room for our first dance. It was awesome!

We danced to Wet, Wet, Wet's "Love Is All Around". I can still "...feel it in my fingers, I feel it in my toes..."

Eventually we got most everybody at the reception to join us in a conga line and many even attempted to limbo! My college roommate Steve Hoffmann shared a prayer and blessing before we ate. While we ate, Susan's Uncle Michael shared a traditional Irish blessing:

May the road rise up to meet you.

May the wind be always at your back.

May the sun shine warm upon your face;

the rains fall soft upon your fields and until we meet again,

may God hold you in the palm of His hand.

A thespian in his younger days (family rumors were that he studied with actor Danny DeVito at some point), Michael had a flair for the dramatic. He embellished some of the words of the poem. And, that bagpiper from the church? It was his surprise gift to us, but we learned later that when Michael heard the reception had an open bar, he "paid" the piper with an invitation! This, of course, was much to Susan's and her Father's surprise!

We had a DJ named Pete Serpico. As only Susan would know, and then share with everybody who would listen, Pete was a distant relative of Officer Frank Serpico from the 1973 movie of the same name, *Serpico*, made famous by Al Pacino. She was breathlessly telling everybody at the reception that Pete was related to Officer Serpico! Things like that always amused and energized her. Honestly, that type of enthusiasm is contagious.

We honeymooned at Disney. The morning after we arrived we were eating baguettes in a bakery in the French Quarter of Epcot. Susan looked up and saw a variety of coats of arms hanging from the rafters. What did she find? Her new name was on a banner directly above her. As was becoming more and more evident to me, Susan was so in touch with signs like that.

SAINTONGE

Chapter 6
Starting Out in New Hampshire - 1994–1997

Newlyweds, Clerkships and Zoe!

After our wedding and honeymoon we settled into life together in New Hampshire. I was clerking and Susan picked up work as a legal secretary. Soon after, she started what would be a lifelong career in higher education. Her first step was working as an administrator in a graduate degree program at Franklin Pierce College.

Those were both glorious and challenging days. Crippling law school debt limited some of our activity, but we managed to go skiing in the New Hampshire White Mountains and we traveled all over the state spending time with aunts and uncles and cousins. We loved their impromptu visits to our home and enjoyed dropping in on people as well.

Susan befriended two neighbors including a young high school girl named Jennifer Russell (Yearwood). Susan became somewhat of a mentor to her. They would go for walks and talk about the challenges of growing up in a home with younger, very athletic brothers and a demanding police officer father. It was my first glimpse into what kind of mother Susan would become.

Compassionate, great listeners, and ever practical, Susan and Jen, despite their age difference, were great friends. We danced at Jen's first wedding and Susan was so very proud of her, from a distance, when Jen became a mother. Susan always seemed to attract younger people to her side.

Another new friend from the neighborhood went to Weight Watchers with her. Susan was very dedicated to the program and went "lifetime" on it, meaning she reached a previously unattainable goal. The company offered to fly her to Manhattan for a professional photo shoot so she could be featured in their marketing material. They told her she could bring one other person to accompany her for the day-long shoot.

Did she bring the love of her life? Yep, she brought her bestest girlfriend growing up, Susan Letwink. It only bothers me a little, a lifetime later, that she did not ask me to go. That incident pales in comparison to the time I bought her Duran Duran concert tickets and, when I told her to take the person she would have the most fun with, she chose Letwink, again. Sigh… More on her later!

My Susan often had a way of getting what she wanted. She sweet-talked our landlord in New Hampshire into letting us have a dog, in violation of our lease. Somebody had randomly thrown a beer bottle through our big picture window, so she convinced the landlord that we needed a "security dog." What did she get? A 28-pound corgi named Zoe! Security? Huh! She would have licked any intruder to death!

One summer day, I was inside lounging on the couch watching golf or baseball or something where I could hear Susan through an open window taking pictures of Zoe. We had recently acquired this massive block of chocolate from dear friends of ours who worked for the NBA. It was a Nestlé Crunch Bar—super giant—it had to be 18–24 inches long. Susan was trying to take a picture of Zoe juxtaposed against the chocolate bar. I heard her saying to Zoe "...think Big! Be long!"

I mentioned traveling around New Hampshire. Once, Susan and I went to visit my paternal grandmother, Jeanne St.Onge, or, to us, Memere. She lived about three hours away in Berlin, New Hampshire, in the shadow of Mount Washington.

Memere, mother of eight, was like Susan. She was always cheerful, ready with a smile and a compliment. We took her to lunch at the Yokohama Restaurant and Susan started digging for family information as only she could. And, Memere was only too happy to oblige her!

I had told Susan about the long family trips we took with our grandparents. I told her how Memere told family stories for hours at a time on those drives. So, Susan wanted a piece of that! Moreover, Susan thought that Memere looked, spoke and carried herself very much like her paternal grandmother who had passed away years earlier. Suffice it to say, Susan's and Memere's energies absolutely resonated with each other.

Susan was able to ask her questions that I, the second oldest grandchild in the clan, never would have. For example, over fried rice and green tea, Susan innocently inquired, "Memere, I have to ask, eight kids?" Oh boy, I was glad to be in between bites of bok choy because I'm sure I would have coughed it up trying to stifle a nervous laugh.

Nonplussed, and without so much as a raised eyebrow, Memere, a distinguished woman of about 80 at that time, responded simply, "We didn't have television..." We laughed and laughed. Both ladies laughed so hard they had tears of joy in their eyes.

Classic Susan. Classic Memere.

After Susan got Zoe, we introduced her to Memere while at my parents' lake house. Memere went back to Berlin, and with her typical high energy enthusiasm, confounded our extended family by telling them all about Susan and Kevin's "new pet goatee!" (A phone call cleared up the matter—*corgi*). That was also around the time she was excited to tell everybody about visiting the lake house and going "cow whacking." Um, she meant kayaking! God bless you Memere. You were so naturally vibrant and funny.

Susan loved those stories.

As wonderful as life was, we also faced challenges and tragedies.

While skiing at Waterville Valley with my college roommate and the dude who sang at our wedding, Anthony Azzara, Susan tore her ACL and MCL. We had driven Anthony's Jeep Wrangler to the mountain. She could not bend her knee. It made the trip home in the cozy confines of the Jeep somewhat uncomfortable.

A couple of weeks later, knee surgery confined her to a brace for several weeks just before our scheduled trip to Disney with my family. Susan, ever the trooper, was still all in. We got her a wheelchair and capitalized on all of the advantages her condition afforded. Preferred seating at events and venues, cutting lines on rides that she could go on, it was awesome!

We went to Disney's Typhoon Lagoon to go swimming and sliding, but Susan could not participate. True to her character, she told us to go off and have a great time. My extended family of aunts, uncles and some cousins joined us that day so we were a big group of over 30 people. Off we went, leaving Susan sitting at a table with all of our stuff. (We St.Onges are simply too frugal to spend the money to rent day lockers.)

As typical of Disney, a kindly older gentleman working guest relations saw her sitting by herself and went to talk to her. He asked her why she was at a water park, in a brace, as she obviously couldn't play in the park and was sitting alone. As only Susan could do, she befriended the man, and he headed off to go get her some ice cream intending to keep her company and be refreshed.

In the meantime, our group returned to the table at about the same time as the gentleman returned with a clearly insufficient amount of ice cream! Whatever Susan had said to him before, they were clearly fast friends, making him OUR fast friend. He disappeared again to get ALL of us some ice cream! Classic Susan.

We joked about keeping the brace for the next trip, even after she healed, so we could keep getting that royal treatment!

I mentioned tragedy during the New Hampshire years. My sister Sandy had been struggling with mental illness for several years. Susan was a great friend to her. Sandy looked up to her as a big sister. Susan had the natural ability to make a person feel completely at ease with her and open up. Sandy did that in a handwritten letter in 1992 (before Susan and I were engaged). Sandy's letter demonstrated how much pain she was in while also acknowledging Susan's positive presence in her life.

4-15-92   11:42 pm

Dear Sue,

Thanks so much for your phone call tonight. I hope that our friendship will continue to grow and we will become better friends. I'm sure it will happen naturally over time.

I realize the stuff I told you tonight is not unique to me but is a common human experience. Some people feel the agony of self-doubt or the agony of something just as shattering at different points in their lives. I feel strengthened and renewed with hope that there are other people out there strong enough to encourage me and keep me going until I have the stamina and ability to stand up straight and continue forward. I also have the desire and natural inclination (as most other people I'm sure) to encourage other people and support them in any way I can.

I hope to support you Sue with what I can. I love you and I am filled with happiness to see the immense love Kevin has for you. You have helped him in so many ways. He really (well it seems to me!) has been touched and inspired by your friendship.

Whatever course you choose to take, whether it's with or without Kevin, I hope you will be blessed with internal peace always!

Love you Sue!

   Sandy

P.S. The human heart yearns for the beautiful in all ranks of life. Harriet Beecher Stowe

Sadly, on July 25, 1995, in a last act of control, fighting desperately against a schizophrenic form disorder, Sandy took her own life.

Suffice to say, we were devastated. Susan lost her new "sister." We comforted each other through that time and learned a great deal about grief. These lessons would inform me, again, years later.

Sandy, Susan and Sue
Letwink (Howell)

Sandy Ann St.Onge
November 22, 1971 – July
25, 1995

Chapter 7
The Middle Years in New Jersey -
1997–2014(ish)

By 1997, I had completed my clerkship but had difficulty finding other employment in New Hampshire. I had been working for the City of Manchester as the back-up prosecutor in the office, which sucked. I would be called-upon to go to District Court on short notice to try misdemeanor cases and probable cause hearings with no time to talk to witnesses.

Those days stressed me out but Susan gave me amazing support. My best friend and confidant, she helped me keep things in perspective. I was better suited to the work I did on the civil side, representing the City in labor matters, zoning and planning board matters (one of which landed me in the National Enquirer of all things—but we will save that for a different book!).

Susan enjoyed her graduate admissions job at Franklin Pierce College but it required working lots of nights and weekends. That put us back into a long-distance relationship of sorts. Our time together was brief and sporadic. Worse, neither of us were making any money and I had burdensome law school loans to repay.

A Dalton family friend was a senior partner at a mid-sized law firm in New Jersey. Long story short, they made me an offer that almost doubled my City salary. It was never my intention to move to New Jersey but our finances dictated it. Moreover, I could tell Susan was stagnating at her job and missed her New Jersey friends, especially Susan Letwink. Off to New Jersey we went.

She landed a position in the financial aid office at Rutgers University. It was a cesspool of public sector employment (interpret that as you want) and her experience was awful. While she always looked to make friends and find the good in people, Rutgers challenged her high vibrations and natural, positive, disposition.

The move to New Jersey had so many other benefits and I knew it meant more to her than she would ever let on. She missed her family and especially her friends. Remember, this was a time before social media "shrank" the world.

The Internet was accessed via dial up. It was slow and inconsistent. Social media itself was basically born that year when one of the first social networking sites, SixDegrees.com, allowed users to set up a profile and send messages within defined networks. Quaint in comparison to today's social media monsters, I often wonder if we would have made the same decisions if we had Facebook and instant messaging then. Susan, at her core, was a social being and craved connection. Returning to New Jersey allowed her to reconnect directly with childhood friends.

Fortunately, Susan was not at Rutgers very long. She got a job in graduate admissions at a private university, Fairleigh Dickinson University (FDU), located in bucolic Florham Park, New Jersey. She made great, lifelong friends there including her assistant, Kathy Carsillo, and her family.

Susan and Kathy shared an office on campus in a former Vanderbilt Mansion. We had so much fun attending black-tie affairs in the ballroom of that same building each spring. It was so beautiful in fact that when Hollywood Director Ron Howard was making the movie *A Beautiful Mind* with Russell Crowe, they selected the Mansion's ballroom as the location for two night scenes in the movie. If memory serves, it was depicted as the Massachusetts Governor's Mansion.

When the film crew was on campus, someone started a rumor that Crowe would be working out in the university weight room. When the women on campus heard about this, many found their workout clothes and started going to the gym hoping to catch his eye.

Susan scoffed at the notion of wanting to impress Crowe. She told me she was happy with her pale, balding, paunchy, 30-something husband. In response, I teased her "…oddly, I found a gym bag in your car. He was the gladiator after all."

In 2024, Kathy shared her recollection of that time and place with me in a text message.

Those were the days my friend. The office we shared was, back in the Vanderbilt days, a linen closet. I had my daughter's little pink radio that we set up on the very large window sill. It was the only way we could get reception.

We loved the same music even though I was years older than her.

We had so many talks about life, our families, and spouses. She Loved you so much and could not wait to start a family with you.

When they were filming "A Beautiful Mind" we were not allowed in our offices in the Mansion so one day Sue bought a six-pack of beer and we sat on top of a hill nearby and watched all the back-up ladies, extras, that were "going to the ball" in the scene they were shooting, get their hair done etc.

That day I told Sue she better not leave FDU. I Loved her like a sister. Every day, she put a smile on my face.

When Susan moved to a different department and was in charge of organizing the University's black-tie Charter Day event, she was pregnant with Molly. She needed to fill some empty seats. So she called me and Liz Dickovics to fill the seats. We were not typically invited to such high-end events!

We were so excited to be going to The Ball!! No, it wasn't the ball in "A Beautiful Mind" but it was an actual ball in a Vanderbilt Mansion!

We ran home and scrambled through our closets to find the right dresses.

The night began and we danced the night away with Sue, and Molly in her belly! It was one of the best nights. We were Cinderella for the night. Thank you Susan!

Susan was an amazing woman, smart, funny and the best friend a girl could ask for.

One Friday about 10 minutes before quitting time, Don McLean's "American Pie" came on that little pink radio. We both just started dancing and screaming out the lyrics. That song became our 5:00 PM-time-for-the-weekend song!

I wish I could have one more conversation with her.

Love you Susan St. Onge until we meet again.

Anything you need, let me know.

Kathy Carsillo

While Susan was loving her job at FDU, I hated being a junior associate at a private practice law firm. I had been working in the public sector labor area at the City Solicitor's office in New Hampshire but expected to transition to a more lucrative private sector employment litigation practice when I joined the firm in New Jersey. However, my start date coincided with the firm's merger with an attorney who had a large public sector (mostly school districts) practice.

Someone who wasn't involved in my hiring process thought that moving me to a support role for that new partner would be a great idea. Another long story short, I was sold a bill of goods. A year later,

I jumped at the first chance to leave that firm and go back to, of all things, the public sector.

FDU Charter Day (2002)

Chapter 8
Here Come the Girls!

In 1998 joined the New Jersey Public Employment Relations Commission (PERC) as a staff agent and hearing examiner. It was a stable job for about seven years, but, like Susan's experience at Rutgers, in time I came to learn that I simply was not cut out for State employment in New Jersey. However, as with my part-time prosecuting days, Susan was my rock and talked me off the proverbial ledge too many times to count.

It was during those years, as Kathy Carsillo reminded me, that we were able to start our family.

Sometimes we can make chicken soup out of, well, you know, the other stuff.

2002 Molly Maeve

Owing primarily to financial pressures and restraints and career starts and stops, we delayed starting our family until we were both 32 years old. By then we had purchased our house in Fanwood, New Jersey, on a little circle near a park and train line that connected to Manhattan.

Early in the workday on September 11, 2001, I got a phone call from Susan telling me that an airplane had just flown into the World Trade Center. She was across the river at Castle Point, Hoboken, in a high-rise building on the Stevens Institute of Technology campus. She was in her office watching smoke pour out of the WTC. I was not far away in my office in Newark and interpreted what she told me as though it were possibly a small Cessna or something that had some type of mechanical failure. She was adamant that no, this was serious.

It is axiomatic now to say that the world changed on September 11th. It was eerie driving by train stations along the commuter line to Manhattan late at night, in the days following, and seeing cars that were parked that morning never to be picked up by their owners.

I am told, although I have never confirmed, that there was an uptick in the number of babies being born nine to 12 months after the terrorist attack. True or not, that notion resonates with me.

Our roots in Fanwood established, however precariously, along came Molly on June 25, 2002. You do the pregnancy math!

We opted not to know the sex of the baby before delivery, simply looking forward to the surprise. We had a tough time agreeing on names. Susan wanted traditional Irish-American names for boys: Sean, Timothy and the like. For a girl, it would be Maeve. But Susan, raised with two older brothers, anticipated a boy.

On June 24th, Susan went into labor and it lasted for what seemed to be an eternity but was officially about 22 hours. We planned for a natural delivery, but by hour 20 it became clear there was something wrong. The umbilical cord was wrapped around the baby's neck. Natural birthing was no longer an option. Cesarean section it would be. We had a great OB/GYN and surgical team and this beautiful baby girl came screaming into the world in the early morning hours (1:01 AM) of June 25th.

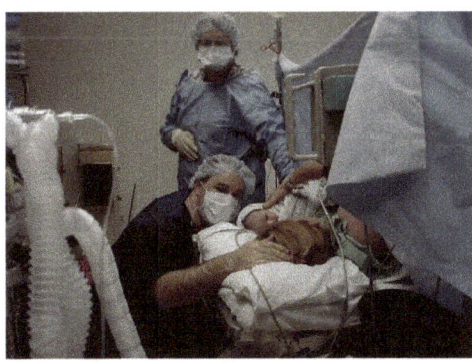

When we saw she was a girl we compromised on Maeve as her middle name. Susan said her first name would be Molly. Given the events of the previous hours I could tell there would be no further discussion. Besides, I love the name. She is, and will always be, my little M&M!

While Susan recovered, she point-blank asked anyone who would listen, "What am I going to do with a girl? I grew up with boys…" She did not have to worry. She was a natural at motherhood. She was born to be one. She often joked that she wanted "three and an oops," and we talked about possibly fostering or adopting later in life if our health and finances allowed. They didn't.

But in 2002 we were over the moon! Molly went everywhere with us. We had a backpack travel seat for her and Susan made sure she was mobile! Molly had the biggest, bluest eyes, just like her Mom. She also had Guinness Book of World Record length eyelashes!

Susan taught me about fatherhood and courage and tried to teach me about patience. I'm still amazed that she let me take 8-month-old Molly on the 5-hour drive to New Hampshire to visit my parents—by myself! Without her! I was petrified! But, if she was nervous, she never showed it. In that way, she showed an implicit trust and faith in me that I'm not sure I ever adequately reciprocated.

I still have no idea what she did that weekend in the quiet of our home without me and Molly. Probably something with Letwink.

2004 Nora Jane

Two years later, on September 1, 2004, we didn't have to be inspired by tragedy to have another child. We wanted Molly to have a sibling and Susan was working on her "three and an oops" plan. I don't remember many details from Susan's pregnancies except that she was very sensitive to certain odors, could not eat chicken (hard for her because she loved it) and she insisted that the babies developing hair in utero made her burp constantly. Oh, and her beer cravings made her proficient at searching for good non-alcoholic beers. Despite her best efforts, as a second generation Irish-American, I'm not sure she ever found a non-alcoholic beer that she could really accept.

Again, we opted for surprise and did not know the sex before delivery. In contrast to Molly's delivery, this one was as uneventful as having a baby could be. Susan was fond of saying how much she appreciated that Nora let her walk in for a scheduled (9:00 AM) C-section. Nora came right on time (something she now struggles with!). Molly had a little sister!

Delivery was the easy part. Parenting a 2-year-old and a newborn, at the same time, well, that was something else entirely. To borrow some sports analogies, with one, we had the option to single-cover or double-team her. With two, we were committed to a zone defense.

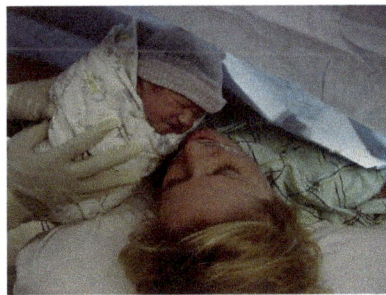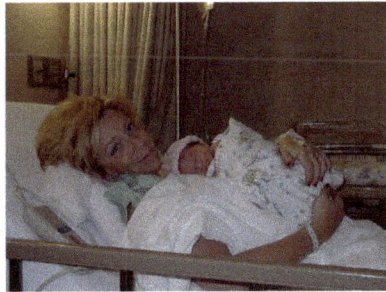

During those 5 years, our little family did what little families do. We celebrated birthdays and holidays. We went on vacations, typically to Lake Winnipesaukee in New Hampshire and Manasquan in New Jersey to share our girls with their respective grandparents. Disney, the Outer Banks of North Carolina, Williamsburg, and Gettysburg were other destinations.

It was also during that time that I left PERC and, following a brief but miserable stint at a large law firm (another New Jersey cesspool of obnoxiousness I could not stomach), I joined my parent's New Hampshire-based company, Johnson Precision, Inc. I worked remotely from my basement in New Jersey trying to drum-up manufacturing sales for my folks. At about the same time, I opened The St.Onge Law Firm.

Susan was my biggest cheerleader, particularly as it related to the law firm. She knew how much it meant to me to build something for myself. She pitched in when and where she could. But, mostly, she kept the domestic life as light and fun and healthy for our family as possible.

It was not long after Nora was born that Susan wanted number three! Unfortunately, that was easier said than done. For a variety of reasons, we could not get pregnant. It took five years, and, regrettably, several miscarriages. Susan was devastated, physically and emotionally, with each loss. Her natural good cheer was severely tested in those days.

Susan was never one to be down for long though. We rallied together and by early 2009, about to turn 40 years old, we were pregnant again! Given our recent history of losing pregnancies, it was too early to share our great news. We kept it confidential.

Another thing I kept confidential was that I was covertly planning a surprise 40th birthday party for Susan!

Susan's 40th Birthday Bash!

Happy Birthday
Susan
We Love You!

February 10, 2009, would be Susan's 40th birthday. January 31, 2009, however, was the date of her surprise birthday bash! My to-do list looked like this:

Banquet room at a local hotel - ✓

Several slideshow videos set to music - ✓

Harpist to play '80s music for Susan - ✓

Homemade little stage or "pedestal" - ✓

Set up room as a "theater in the round" - ✓

Projector screen for the slides - ✓

Podium (I love me a good podium!) - ✓

70+/- friends and family members - ✓

Always a fan of the celebrity roast, I planned a "Susan Roast" to take place after the happy hour.

I told Susan that I had planned a date night as a ruse to get her to the party. The kids were already with my parents at the hotel so we just had to stop in to check on them before going on to our dinner. On our way over, she complained that she was starving and couldn't wait to eat. Thoughts of hunger left her mind after walking into the room, though! She was absolutely surprised! We got her!

She was so swept up in the moment, jibber-jabbering with all her favorite people, that she never even got to taste the hors d'oeuvres served during the cocktail hour. Remember, she was about a month, plus or minus, pregnant and we had not told anyone. She was not drinking alcohol and was instead ordering Shirley Temples with the kids. Her pregnancy bladder was rapidly filling but she just could not get away to the Ladies room. Then, the Roast started and she sat on her pedestal and listened to the roasters and watched the videos—later telling me that all she could focus on was not peeing her pants every time she laughed. Somehow, her bladder issues became my fault!

For many years, all I heard about was how hungry she was that night (we never made it to dinner!) and how badly she had to pee! While she never did ask for such a big party, I know she absolutely loved being the center of attention that time. We had so much fun that night with our parents, our children (although the baby who would become Ella was still in utero!) and our dearest friends. Some of the more discerning women there took note of the fact that Susan was not drinking alcohol and later said they "just knew" she must have been pregnant!

2009 Ella Claire

Ella was due in late October, 2009, but she couldn't wait that long! I was playing basketball on what had become a regular Thursday night run with the Father's Club guys at Mount Saint Mary Academy just up the hill from our home. I should not have been playing: 40 years old, way out of shape, I had a lot of "go" but not a lot of "woah," so I kept spraining my ankles. Three third degree ankle sprains in four years convinced me to give it up and become a referee instead, but that is a different story for a different book.

Susan was trying to reach me while I was on the court to say that she was experiencing some unusual discomfort and wanted me to come home early. I didn't realize I had missed calls until I was heading home and checked my messages en route. When I got home I guess I missed the signals that she was in distress because I made the mistake of asking her if I could grab a shower before we left for the hospital. All these years later I can still remember her furious raised eyebrow. Fortunately for me, one of our bestest neighborhood friends, Mike Taylor, was there to take the two older girls to the Taylor house down the street for the night!

Off to Overlook Hospital in Summit, New Jersey, we went. We thought the baby was still baking in there but Susan's intuition about what required a trip to the hospital was never wrong. She always knew when she, or a member of her family, needed medical attention. For example, both Molly and Ella broke their arms. The fractures were so slight and they did not present as classic breaks.

Susan was sure that something was wrong but I was skeptical. I was proven wrong both times! Susan was also the voice of reason to get Ella to the hospital when she developed certain food allergies at about age six, but I am getting ahead of the Ella part of the story!

Back to 2009, once again, Susan was right. The baby was early. Viable, but early. We got to the hospital and Susan was prepped for another C-section. At 10:53 PM on October 8, 2009, another beautiful baby girl came crying into the world! We named her Ella Claire. Susan convalesced while I spent time with the maternity nurses bathing Ella and giving her her first shampoo. She had a lot of hair!

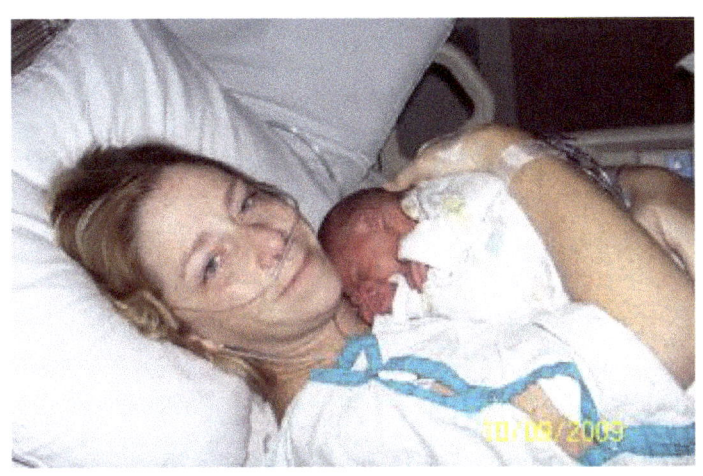

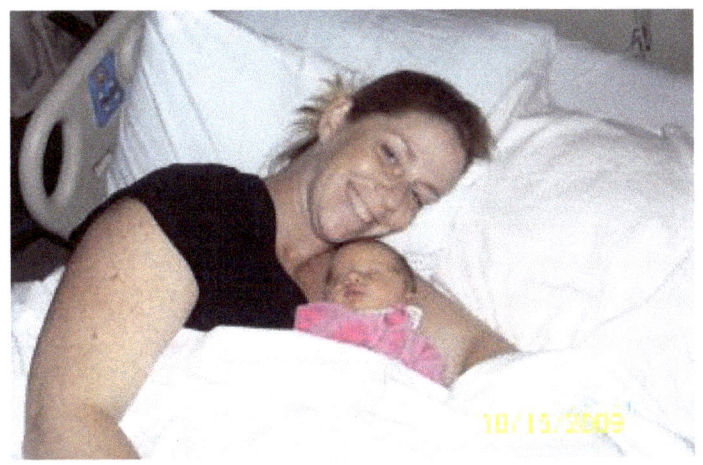

Chapter 9
Susan's Near Death Experience

A few hours after Ella was born, she was getting a suntan, warming under the heat lamps in the nursery. Susan was in a private room sleeping. I was dozing in a chair next to her when, at approximately 7:00 AM, she flailed an arm at me and called my name. She said she could not see, or that she had "kaleidoscope" vision and that she felt like her head would explode. I pressed the call button and just as the nurse walked in Susan began seizing.

If you have ever seen a person have a full-on seizure then you know how scary it can look. Susan's eyes rolled back and her body convulsed involuntarily to the point she almost fell out of the bed. She looked possessed like in those '80s horror movies she liked. The nurse immediately called in a code blue and within seconds the room filled with every doctor on trauma-team duty in the hospital. I was squished up against a windowsill and had a birds-eye view of the melee that was occurring before me. It was semi-controlled chaos as one particular doctor took control of the situation and began barking out commands like a quarterback.

I wish I knew the names of the people in the room. I hope I come across the list of their names in Susan's papers some day. I'm fairly sure she wrote them down and kept it.

I have forgotten (or maybe blocked) the medical terms and procedures they used to bring Susan back from that seizure but I remember Susan saying later that she most definitely had a near death experience (NDE). She was heading down a long, dark, tunnel towards a light. She heard a voice telling her it was not time for her to go and she felt two arms pulling her back. The voice and the arms belonged to the quarterback doctor who was standing near her head.

When she was "back" Susan immediately called for me by name, "Kevin! I can't see anything. Are you here?" The chaos calmed slightly, all eyes in the room found me pressed hard against the window trying desperately to stay out of the way. She wasn't out of danger yet. Her blood pressure was through the roof. Her body was barely covered by a hospital gown that was all but torn off her during the seizure. The larger muscles of her arms and legs, visible, were still quivering from the after-effects.

"I'm right here Susan…" I replied in the strongest voice I could muster in the moment. Later, I was told that I could have done a voiceover for Mickey Mouse, my voice was so thin. But, I answered her and the QB Doc looked at me as if to say, "Keep talking to her…" So I did.

"Susan, you're in great hands. The nurses and doctors here are doing everything they can for you. You need to try to calm yourself and focus solely on your breathing. Ella is in the nursery. Molly and Nora are at the Taylor's. You have nothing else in this world to think about right now except doing whatever these people tell you and I will be here the whole time. I am not going anywhere. Close your eyes. Breath and be present. I am right here. I love you."

Those amazing, nameless, Overlook Hospital heroes stabilized my world, my Wife, that day.

She was diagnosed with preeclampsia, although I never understood the word because it happened after delivery, thus was not "pre" anything. We weren't doctors but this is what we learned: postpartum preeclampsia can affect all the organs in a woman's body. It occurs when a woman has high blood pressure and other signs that her organs aren't working normally. Most often, symptoms of preeclampsia happen during pregnancy. But, some women can develop preeclampsia after delivery, even women who may have had normal blood pressure during pregnancy.

A scary thought we learned was that postpartum preeclampsia most often develops within a few days *after* delivery, but it can occur up to six weeks later! I cannot imagine what would have happened had we been at home or if Susan had been alone and not in the hospital. Untreated, preeclampsia can cause stroke, seizures, and other serious problems.

For days afterwards she experienced pressure headaches. We fought hard to get her the care she needed which turned out to be a spinal blood patch, a technique used to rebalance the pressure in the spinal column. That helped, but the worst side effect of the episode was the debilitating high blood pressure. She took meds and almost a year to recover before she started to feel like herself again.

Susan was in the hospital for a couple of weeks after her seizure. I am so grateful that her parents and my parents were there for us. Susan's parents lived locally in New Jersey. They were always willing to take the girls. My parents visited often from New Hampshire and my mother stayed with us during Susan's hospital stay and for the first several weeks after she returned home.

Ella was very colicky. She had a tough time digesting her food. Given Susan's condition, I took the overnight feedings. My Mother often sat up with me or, just as often, she took the overnight feedings. Reflecting on those times now, writing this, it puts a lump in my throat to think about just how fortunate we were that all four of our parents were involved in our lives.

I distinctly remember one particular moment when Susan was still in the hospital. Molly and Nora had not seen their Mother since before the seizure. It was probably a couple of days later and "Booma," as the girls called Susan's Mom, and my Mother (Grammy) brought them to the hospital so they could visit. We agreed that Molly and Nora would not meet Ella until we could do it as a family. I think this was that day. But, first, Molly and Nora were going to visit their Mother in her hospital room. Both Grandmothers were standing in a dark and super quiet hallway. The hospital placed Susan in a really quiet wing of the maternity ward.

Molly, age seven, and Nora, age five, had clearly been prepped by their Grandmothers to be "as quiet as church mice." I remember kneeling down in the hallway so that I could look them in the eyes and prepare them for what they would see when they went in the room. Mommy would be laying in bed. It would be dark and her eyes might be closed, but she was definitely awake and she absolutely wanted to see her girls. They had to promise to use their "inside voices" and make sure that only one person was talking at a time.

I asked the Grandmothers to wait in the visitor's lounge while I took each girl by the hand and we walked the 50 or so feet to the closed door of Susan's private room. I remember thinking at that moment just how lucky we were that Susan survived the seizure because I could've been holding my daughters' hands and walking them to a funeral home. Little did I know that nine years later that was exactly what we would be doing.

Chapter 10
Recovery, Loss and Moving Family Forward

Susan was home for about a month. Recovery was slow. Her blood pressure remained high. We modified the routines in our house, which was no easy task with active seven and five-year-olds! But one of our girls wasn't doing so well. Zoe, our beloved dog, was declining. She had been with us through the move to New Jersey, the purchase of the house, all of the job changes, and not one, not two, but now three babies!

She was a trooper through it all! Corgis are known for their loyalty. And, although sometimes a little yappy, their instinct is to herd. It was so much fun to watch her "herd" her herd, Molly and Nora, around our little house! She would sleep on the floor next to the crib or under their beds. She was a great dog but her health was failing.

I don't remember why, but I was a jerk.

Despite Susan's condition that Fall, it somehow fell on her to take Zoe to the Fanwood Animal Hospital and have her euthanized. I honestly don't remember why I didn't do that. For that, I am eternally sorry. Zoe's remains were cremated and returned to us in a little wooden box that Susan made sure sat in a place of honor in one of our curio cabinets. She is still there among so many other memories.

In addition to all that, I didn't know it at the time, but that Fall of 2009 my parents were in the process of selling their company, Johnson Precision, Inc. As hard as it was for my Mother to be away from New Hampshire and my Father during that time, she knew that my little family needed her. I needed her. I'm so grateful. I will always be grateful to her for being there for us. Thank you, Mom!

Stop, Family Time… (Yes, another '80s reference!)"

I showed Susan how much I loved her by working hard as a partner in the care of our daughters. There is no question that Susan changed more diapers and gave more "tubbies" than I did, but I was very involved. I was probably better at swaddling them as babies and she was certainly better at diaper work. We made a great team!

As I mentioned, I typically had the overnights. I loved how our babies felt when they were tiny and could lay on their bellies on the inside of my forearm with their chins resting between my fingers. I found that to be the most effective way to burp them after feeding. It was so satisfying when you tapped their little butts and you just felt them burp up their gas. You could feel their relief! I did that with all three girls. Susan taught me how to do it!

I distinctly remember Susan made it a point to wake up every morning in a good mood. She tried to instill that in her daughters. All four of us remember hearing her say some variation of "happy good morning sunshine!"

Susan used to love to sing a variety of songs to her girls, but most commonly "You Are My Sunshine". I have a little plaque in our kitchen with the words to it. The final verse to it still puts a lump in my throat, "…please don't take my Sunshine away…" That song inspired Nora to write her own sunshine song variation about Susan simply titled "My Sunshine". She released it to Spotify on Susan's birthday, February 10, 2024.

It was Susan who made sure that our two older girls played softball through eighth grade. All three played soccer and I coached, at least through kindergarten. Once I realized that coaching for that age group was akin to herding cats, and I was out of my depth, I stepped aside. Ella was probably the best soccer player in the family and had her best season during Susan's final spring with us. It was also Ella's final season of soccer.

Susan was always looking for ways for us to all have fun. On one trip to the Gettysburg Battlefield, we dressed up in period attire and took a family photo that became our Christmas card that year!

Early in their lives, Susan made sure that our children told us what things they were interested in doing. Molly found horseback riding and playing the saxophone, eventually earning a spot in the middle school jazz band. She went on to participate in an award-winning high school marching band that took her to the fields of several cool stadiums including MetLife Stadium and Rutgers Stadium. Her marching band even paraded down Main Street in Disney World! My Mom captured the coolest picture of Molly having the time of her life in that parade!

Nora found her voice, quite actually, when she was six or seven years old. She was singing a duet of "Blessed Be The Lord" with her sister in our living room and the two were harmonizing quite nicely. It quickly became evident that Nora had a natural ear for music. Susan teamed her up with a voice coach, Mary Lou Farrell, and her music career was born! She sang in the middle school chorus and jazz band. She played the flute. She joined the color guard in high school.

Molly Marching at Disney

Susan and Nora
Manasquan, New Jersey
July 2, 2006

Of the three, Nora looks most like Susan. Although all our girls
share various characteristics with their Mother, Nora probably comes

closest as our middle. When she was four or five years old, she somehow got her hands on some matches and was in the bathroom lighting Kleenex or toilet paper on fire and throwing them in the air because she thought they looked like "fireflies" fluttering through the air. She almost burned the house down that Christmas! As I said, very Susan-like.

Susan sent the older girls to Girl Scout Camp, two hours away in the middle of Nowhere, Pennsylvania. Molly promptly injured herself by falling off a horse and we thought we would have to go pick her up. We didn't, she toughed that one out! And, although Nora complained she didn't have a lot of fun, we could tell just how much fun they really had by how badly they stank on the ride home from Pennsylvania!

During those years, Ella was our little nugget. Five and seven years younger than her sisters, we towed her around to all of their events and she learned by "watching the big kids."

Ella is a quick study. At around 18 months old, wearing a diaper but no shirt or shoes, she climbed out of her crib. Susan, the older girls and I were in the garage preoccupied with something. Ella was supposed to be napping, but she found her way out of the crib, out of her room, out of the house and across the street to Kathy and Brian Maloney's house. Apparently when Brian saw this 18-month-old in a diaper playing with his dog, he asked Kathy "...um, should she be here?"

When Kathy brought her over, we were mortified, petrified and so grateful all at once! Susan asked Ella "where were you going?" Ella responded in her little girl voice "...the puppy needed to be petted..."

Our little family had so much fun. We went to the lake, we went to the beach. We took the girls skiing. We celebrated birthdays in our local LaGrande Park Pavilion. Susan made sure they took dance lessons at the YMCA. They participated in the various little shows put on by their elementary and middle schools.

They all had amazing teachers in elementary and middle school and beyond. Susan made sure to stay connected to the girls' classrooms and all of their academic needs. She even volunteered her time to bake cookies and brownies for bake sales. She did much of this while working a full-time job (before Ella, that is). She took some time off after the seizure episode, but she did go back to work and manage to juggle daycare, a full-time job and Motherhood.

One of the many jobs she had was at Stevens Institute of Technology working in graduate admissions. Those years brought Susan and her Father closer together than in any other period since her youth. John is a 1961 graduate of Stevens. And Susan knew just how proud he was of his alma mater. As of this writing, he is still very active with his alumni association and fraternity. Occasionally, she stepped in as his "date" to alumni events, particularly the black-tie affairs.

At Stevens, Susan worked in a high-rise building located on Castle Point in Hoboken, New Jersey. As the name implies, it is a point that juts out into the Hudson River directly across from Chelsea in Manhattan. One year, we were able to get window seats on the river side of the building to watch Operation Sail, which was a regatta of majestic three-masted ships sailing their way up the Hudson River. It was beautiful.

Recall, it was here that Susan called me on September 11, 2001, to tell me that an airplane had hit the World Trade Center. Susan was also in that building when Captain Chesley "Sully" Sullenberger landed US Airways Flight 1549 ("Cactus 1549") in the Hudson River. The Airbus A320 lost both engines due to a bird strike shortly after takeoff from LaGuardia Airport. Captain Sully saved all 155 people on board. Susan remembers seeing the plane float by Castle Point and she watched the water rescue effort that followed.

It was during her Stevens days that she befriended another young woman. Much like her impromptu friendship with our neighbor Jennifer Russell years earlier, she became friends with Tracey Ryan (McCarrick). Tracey was a student employee in the admissions office and is probably one of the smartest people I know. Susan saw that immediately and claimed her as her student assistant! Tracey was commuting to Hoboken from Clark, New Jersey, which was right on the way of Susan's commute into work. They started driving in together and a family friendship was born that lasts to this day.

Tracey went onto a career as a pharmaceutical company executive. Before she rose to that level, however, she worked for The St. Onge Law Firm as my bookkeeper/legal assistant/researcher/editor. I don't know what her IQ is, but my guess is that it's off the charts.

Beyond her intelligence, she is incredibly engaging, down to earth and frankly one of the best people I know. She babysat our girls and invited them to her wedding even though they were very young at the time. To this day, Tracey has helped me with various projects and she has kept in touch with our daughters. No matter the time, distance, or lag between calls, she and her husband Craig are among my favorite people in the world and I have Susan to thank for that connection.

Chapter 11
The Two Sues

I've mentioned throughout this book Susan's special connection to Susan Letwink Howell (hereafter referred to as "Letwink" for ease of distinction between the two Sues).

My Susan was two years old, then living on Dorian Court, when Letwink was born. Letwink lived diagonally across the street. (Speaking of "diagonally," my Susan was so proud of herself when she told me that Diagon Alley from the *Harry Potter* series was actually a play on the word "diagonally." She loved that stuff!) Anyway, my Susan used to tell me she remembered Letwink as an infant. I find that hard to believe given how young she was at the time, but she insisted she had memories of baby Letwink.

More believable were the stories about how they used to roller skate in the Letwink's basement, without helmets or kneepads of course! They grew up together in every way possible. They shared major life experiences, celebrating each other's birthdays, holidays, personal victories, tragedies and losses. Godmothers to each other's children (our Molly and Letwink's Sean), the two Sues share a special bond.

My Susan used to love to share neighborhood stories. Letwink's Father, Wayne, was a little hard of hearing. As a result, he was known in the neighborhood for having a booming voice. My Susan used to imitate him and it always made Letwink laugh.

Susan loved that Mr. Letwink was a meticulous notetaker when it came to restaurants all over New Jersey, particularly the Jersey Shore. He had a three ring binder with menus and his own personal review of each spot. Anytime he heard somebody was going to a restaurant, he would say "wait a minute" and run to go get his binder. Oftentimes he didn't even need the binder; he could recite his review from memory.

Mr. Letwink and his wife Judy were career teachers. Wayne became a New Jersey High School Hall of Fame track and field coach and official. Suffice to say, the Letwink family made a lifetime impression on my Susan. She loved them dearly and I believe the feeling was reciprocated.

Letwink was my Susan's Maid of Honor at our wedding. Although, we did not call her a "Maid of Honor." I dubbed her the "Hag of Honor" and that name has stuck! All these years later, it has simply been shortened to "Hag"—at least that is what comes up on my phone when she calls or texts me!

Later, Letwink returned the favor and asked my Susan to be her "Hag of Honor." Susan was all too happy to serve in that capacity. Her favorite responsibility was preparing for her Hag of Honor toast to the married couple. Letwink married a man's man, a manly sort of man, a guy's guy as it were. Brad Howell is one of those Bunyan-esque, get your hands dirty, do it yourself, jack of all trades kind of dudes. Susan used that tableau as the metaphor for her toast at the Howell reception.

Susan borrowed a pair of safety goggles and my leather tool belt. She filled the tool belt with various devices she dubbed "the tools of marriage." I can still picture her in her Maid of Honor gown, all dudded-up, putting on the safety glasses, donning the tool belt and forging ahead with a very risqué toast!

Her comments included references to nuts and bolts to "hold things together" and sandpaper to "smooth things over during the rough times." I don't recall the other PG-rated tools but I know she bravely included references to screwdrivers and hammers for, well, I think you can use your imagination.

Her best advice for a devout bachelor like Brad was to "always leave the toilet seat down." For both of them, she suggested they "...never go to bed angry, but if you are angry, go to bed alone and make the other one stay up and think about what they did wrong."

At first, I was concerned Brad might be too serious and mature to enjoy the two Sues' kind of humor. Thankfully, it elicited at least a smirk. If he didn't like it, I was scared to think of how badly he could have kicked my butt!

Gentle giant that Brad is, my Susan was so happy for her very bestest friend in the whole-wide-world that she found a man to love and have a family with.

Letwink may remember that at the Celebration of Life I said the following,

I can't do your friendship/relationship justice in this little time.
And we don't need to do this publicly. We have and will continue

to talk privately about our Susan. But for now my message to you is that she so loved you and cherished your friendship and wants nothing but peace and happiness for you. And she fully expects you to be a dominant presence in her daughters' lives. Thank you Sue for being her friend. I am so sorry for your loss.

For her part, Letwink honored Susan at the luncheon following the Celebration of Life with the following recollection:

Susan and I first met as very young kids, me as an infant, and she as a two-year year-old, when my family moved across the street from her on Dorian Court. We were called Big Sue and Little Sue, names that carried on almost 47 years later. During that time we acted as the sister to each other that neither of us had...playing paper dolls, sharing clothes, and later my first wine cooler in her attic and dancing to "You Can Call Me Al."

She tried to teach me how to drive, and I almost crashed her car into the project building at WHS, but that's another story. I didn't know you were supposed to drive with just one foot and had my left foot on the brake but still my right on the gas. That was her first and last driving lesson for me.

I would visit her in college and later she would visit me. Sometimes she didn't even tell me she was coming, just told my housemates she was coming to surprise me. One morning (early afternoon) I woke up to her dog Sandy running in my bedroom.

Later on I stood next to her on her wedding day, and then she stood next to me, on mine... I saved mementos from my wedding but I threw out all of the response cards except one—I'll share it with you.

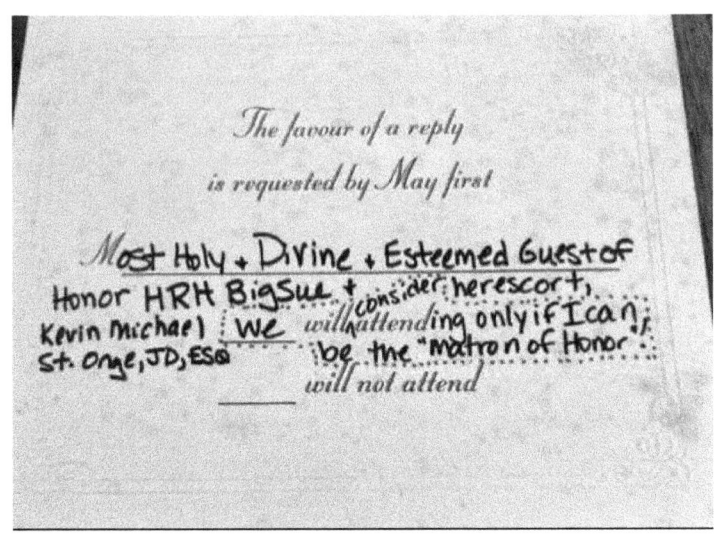

The favour of a reply
is requested by May first

Most Holy + Divine + Esteemed Guest of
Honor HRH BigSue + consider herescort,
Kevin Michael We will attending only if I can
St. Onge, JD, ESQ be the "matron of Honor"
will not attend

Through the years I always looked up to her. Younger girls do look up to older girls, that is true, but there was always something about her that made me want to be just like her. Whatever Susan did, she had fun. Wherever she went, she made friends. She had so much positivity about her, and such a magnetic personality, that it made everyone like her and want to be around her. Such a quick wit, such a sense of humor, she would make me roll on the floor laughing.

I can remember back in 2014, after one of her surgeries, driving her around to run errands. We went to the post office. The guy behind the desk looked bored, just having a regular kind of day at work, the kind we all know too well. He said to Susan in a flat voice, "can I help you?" Sue looked right back at him and said "Hey! How are you DOIN?" She sounded like Joey Tribbiani from "Friends." The guy smiled a smile that went right to his eyes and I remember thinking, "That's my friend… She just makes everyone happy."

I can say with the utmost sincerity that Susan had more fun in her 49 years, and made people more happy in her 49 years, than most people would ever do in a hundred years or more. I think she knew the secret of life happiness comes from helping others. I'm going to try to remember that more and practice that more often so I can honor her in some small way.

Her examples were simple. I saw her take her coat off in winter and put it around a girl she didn't even know to keep her warm coming home from a college party. I learned that while she was working at one of the colleges, she made sure a young boy, who passed away in his 20s, received his diploma posthumously. She tirelessly spent so much of her life just being good to people.

The best part was she didn't let you know she did these things. She let others notice on their own if they wanted to.

It comforts me that Susan left us, not one, but, three little legacies to live on in her spirit. Kevin said he has three little Susan Dalton St.Onges and I see that.

The other night I was over there and Kevin wondered out loud if he needed anything from the store. Molly and Nora said, almost in unison, "hair!" And then, just a beat later, even eight year old Ella chimed in and said the same! I thought, "Wow, Susan is still, and will always be, with us."

In closing, I'd like to recite a few lines from a song from a Broadway show that I believe sums up what Susan was, and always will be, to me.

It may be

That we will never meet again

In this lifetime

So let me say before we part

So much of me

Is made of what I learned from you

You'll be with me

Like a handprint on my heart

And now, whatever way our stories end

I know you have rewritten mine

By being my friend

Like a ship blown from its mooring

By a wind off the sea

Like a seed dropped from a sky bird

Into a distant wood

Who can say if I've been changed for the better

But, because I know you

I have been changed for good

Excerpted from the song "For Good" from the Broadway soundtrack for *Wicked*.

Chapter 12
Random Recollections

Susan taught me about her earlier days, often. I learned about her family, her parents and her brothers.

She told me about growing up in Westfield on Dorian Court, not more than two blocks away from the high school. She taught me about her favorite kindergarten and elementary school teachers. We went to a Livingston Taylor concert at Westfield High School one time and she had to show me where her high school locker had been. It was no longer there, replaced by something, but she still remembered the combination.

Anytime we drove around Westfield, indeed all of New Jersey, Susan had either been there, done that, or had a dream or premonition or even just a "sense" that she had been there!

She told me about working long weekends as a dance instructor in high school.

Every conversation about her friends began with a list of names and who dated who and how long they dated and what happened and somehow they all connected together in some grand scheme or pattern that clearly only she knew and found ironic.

She was fond of talking about how she was born in Chicago, Illinois, and lived there until about age two, before the family moved to Westfield. In the early 2010s, I had business in Illinois so Susan came with me and insisted that we find the house that she and her parents had lived in. As only Susan can do, she knocked on the door, introduced herself to the current owners and became instant friends with them.

I was sitting in the car when I saw her disappear into the house. Now, mind you, we didn't know these people. But when they asked

Susan if she knew about the "ghosts" in the house, she had to go check it out!

She insisted on a ghost tour of Chicago while we were there. In fact, she insisted on ghost tours on almost every trip we went on! That was her jam! She was so fond of the supernatural. She loved to watch all of the TV shows that she could find on the subject.

Always open. Joyful. After she passed, I learned that the word "joy" is an acronym.

J ust

O pen

Y ourself.

It fits Susan perfectly.

On that same trip to Chicago, we had to find the church where she was baptized and light a candle. She always lit candles in churches on any trip we went on! Whether it was St. Patrick's Cathedral in New York City, or Our Lady of Victory Chapel in Center Harbor, New Hampshire, Susan lit candles wherever she went!

She told me about all of her hijinks as a child with her cousins. She was connected with cousins on both her maternal and paternal side. There were always stories about two uncles in particular who supposedly hocked their Mother's stereo to pay for a ride to Woodstock in 1969. Those same two brothers were supposed to be helping Susan's parents move into their home in Westfield that weekend!

She loved to tell stories about her uncle Paul (her Father's brother), who was very much a hippie in his day but died young while living in a commune.

I spent some time with her uncle Edward, who was her Father's twin brother. He had multiple sclerosis. While I don't know all of the details of the story, it was from him that I learned about Medicaid spend-down planning to preserve assets of an existing estate for the beneficiary.

It is still a concept that I find difficult to reconcile.

Our federal government basically established a process that encourages people to impoverish themselves in order to be eligible for federal benefits while preserving their assets for their beneficiaries. To be clear, I don't blame Edward or his family for benefiting by compliance with existing law. I just think the concept is/was poor public policy.

Another healthcare policy change, the Affordable Care Act (ACA) is poor public policy. It impacted us directly in the middle of Susan's second round of chemotherapy. It caused quite a bit of upset in our household when she had to change infusion centers because we were forced, by the ACA, to change insurance carriers thus disrupting her specific treatment plan. Though it made sense to help the uninsured population, it struck me as harsh that we were deprived of coverage we had already paid for because the ACA forced changes in our existing insurance.

Susan's father John and his twin brother Edward were both Stevens Institute of Technology scholarship students from just down the road in Jersey City where they grew up. Susan knew many of the stories from their heyday at Stevens, including supposedly going on double dates and switching dates to see if they could tell them apart!

Susan loved being in Hoboken. Although we lived in the very suburban Borough of Fanwood, she loved the pace and energy of Hoboken. She loved to purchase real Italian "mutz," as she called it, mozzarella cheese to the rest of the world!

Speaking of which, she was an excellent cook. She had a number of go-to dishes both for her and I and also for the kids. Lighter fare for the summer, dense protein-rich foods for the winter. One of my biggest regrets in our life together was that I was unable to provide her with a kitchen commensurate with her talent and desire to cook.

Early in our relationship, it was important to Susan that I meet her maternal grandfather. Grandfather Millman had played minor league baseball way back in the day. By the time I met him he was in very rough shape. Virtually blind, severely hard of hearing, he was confined to his bed in a care facility. It was heartbreaking to see anyone in that condition, but when he heard Susan's voice, instantly recognizable to him, a smile immediately spread across his face. He knew his granddaughter. I was so honored that she included me in that time with him.

Another family story from that maternal Millman side was that her great-great-great-grandfather fought in the Civil War. On a couple trips to Gettysburg, we made sure that we found his name on the Pennsylvania monument. On one particular trip, we made sure to find where his regiment was stationed on each day of the battle. I enjoyed reading some of the original paperwork regarding his enlistment and his family's battles with the federal government seeking veterans benefits afterwards. Apparently, the federal government did not want to pay him retirement benefits because he lied about his age to enter the military. He was too young to enlist, initially serving as a drummer boy. His benefits were eventually reinstated. We have family pictures of Susan and the girls pointing out his name on the monument at Gettysburg. It's a connection to the past that Susan was very proud of.

Other random recollections include Susan's hangover cure:

- Flat Coca Cola

- Quarter pounder with cheese from McDonald's

- Salty french fries

During remission, Susan competed in two or three triathlons and then got into road races, typically 5Ks. She loved to run them with her father and cousin Matthew Shafer. For several years they ran the annual Spring Lake Five together as part of Team Freedom.

Susan loved to have fun and her creativity in that area was unparalleled. She loved taking weird pictures of herself and her friends in funny situations. Who brings women into the men's room? That would be Susan. One common "pose" was to get a bunch of girlfriends and take a group shot of them all standing at urinals in the men's room at weddings.

She also loved to play at "stealing" the centerpieces at weddings. At one wedding, or maybe several, she and my cousin Tracy Ingersoll enjoyed "stealing" salt and pepper shakers, utensils and other small items and putting them in my Aunt Lou's (Tracy's Mom) handbag.

Susan was an adventurous soul. She loved to travel. Typically, though, she did not like to fly. She would do it, but it took a lot. I upgraded us to first class for our honeymoon. More often, we flew coach and I needed to get her a drink (or several) before she got on the plane. When I say white knuckle flier, I mean that quite actually. She gripped my hand so tight it hurt!

Susan's toast when out drinking: "Here's to being single, seeing double and sleeping triple." While I know she was single before we met, and may have seen double a few times, I am fairly sure "sleeping triple" was not an aspiration.

She loved to change the wording of old sayings. For example, the oft-used Irish phrase "Erin go Bragh," loosely meaning "Ireland forever," to Susan was, "Erin go braghless!"

I mentioned elsewhere in this book that she was also familiar with Scranton, Pennsylvania, just down the road from Wilkes-Barre. As adults, Susan sometimes scheduled weekends away for us to go to Scranton for various shows or concerts. Our favorite was a Christmas concert by pianist Jim Brickman. Susan and I seemed to enjoy pianists. We saw Robin Spielberg at Carnegie Hall and in a private garden party venue in Montclair, New Jersey, for Mother's Day one year.

Speaking of Wilkes, Susan submitted the following letter to the Wilkes University Newsletter, published in January, 2006.

This past fall, my family's vacation took a detour through Wilkes-Barre, Pennsylvania. We had not really planned to visit but we followed our instinct. Actually, I was driving and my husband had no choice, however, that is a different story!

Anyway, on a beautiful, September afternoon, I was a cliché – visiting campus and the old stomping grounds with my children (and reluctant husband). We strolled down the path behind Stark Learning Center and I noticed how much had changed. I bought various Wilkes' stuff from the bookstore – the former Pickering/Dining Hall. My favorite purchase was a pink Wilkes' baseball cap – I am a Jersey girl after all! We lunched at the Chicken Coop. Is there any better place for wings? Afterwards, we wandered over to the soccer field to watch the women's team play.

The Wilkes' women's soccer team has come a very, very long way since it was formed. I should know, as I was a freshman that year – 1987! It is hard for me to comprehend that this year's freshman class were born the year the program was formed!

I love soccer. Big fan. I loved playing it and enjoy watching it. By far, the most fun I ever had in the sport was my four years on the Wilkes' team. Watching them play this year brought it all back to me...

Those early years of the program were rough. We were not a winning team – unpolished to say the least. We were, however, hard-working, dedicated and enjoyed the sport enough to show up for practice everyday, week-after-week, even when we knew the odds of us winning the next game were slim-to-none. Looking back now, you could say we were pioneers, but at the time we were just teenage girls having a blast doing something we loved.

Now, almost 20 years later, the team has players being named All-Americans, winning conference titles, and shopping for conference title rings.

WOW! I can't help but feel that everyone who was part of the program in those early days, and every year since, should be proud of where the program is today.

Standing on the sidelines this past September, watching a group of young women having a blast doing something I loved, really brought me back but it also caused me to look ahead. My two daughters (ages 3 and 1) were with me and were wide-eyed with enthusiasm. They were looking up to the players like they were rock stars. When my husband told them I used to play on that same field, they looked at me that way too! It was the coolest thing.

It got better. As we stood on the sidelines talking to several of the players' parents my one-year old decided to pick that moment to take her first steps! I really think she wanted to play!

I was so proud and happy to share my memories with my daughters while celebrating another Wilkes' win!

time to over 44 arms to embrace you when you need it more than you ever thought possible. My time as a Wilkes Women's Soccer player has been a ride. You take out what you give in and to us, it's all about commitment.

Susan Dalton Checks In

This past fall, my family's vacation took a detour through Wilkes-Barre, Pennsylvania. We had not really planned to visit but we followed our instinct. Actually, I was driving and my husband had no choice, however, that is a different story!

Anyway, on a beautiful, September afternoon, it was a cliché – visiting campus and the old stomping grounds with my children (and reluctant husband). We strolled down the path behind Stark Learning Center and I noticed how much had changed. I bought various Wilkes' sundries from the bookstore (my favorite is a pink baseball cap). Afterwards, we wandered over to the soccer field to watch the women's team play.

The Wilkes' women's soccer team has come a very, very long way since it was formed. I should know, I was a freshman that year – 1987! It is hard for me to comprehend that this year's freshman class were born the year the program was formed!

I love soccer. Big fan. I loved playing it and enjoy watching it. By far, the most fun I ever had in the sport was my four years on the Wilkes' team. Watching them play this year brought it all back to me...

Those early years of the program were rough. We were not a winning team – unpolished to say the least. We were, however, hardworking, dedicated and enjoyed the sport enough to show up for practice everyday, week after week, even when we knew the odds of us winning the next game were slim-to-none. Looking back now, you could say we were pioneers, but at the time we were just a bunch of girls having a blast doing something we loved.

Now, 18 years later, the team has traveled to Europe, players being named All-Americans, winning conference titles, and shopping for conference title rings. WOW! I can't help but feel that everyone who was part of program in those early days, and every year since, should be proud of where the program is today.

Standing on the sidelines

this past September, watching a group of young women having a good time doing something I loved, really brought me back, but it also caused me to look ahead. My two daughters (ages 3 and 1) were with me and were wide-eyed with enthusiasm. My 3 year-old was looking up to the players like they were rock stars. When my husband told her I used to play on that same field, she looked at me that way, too! It was the coolest thing.

It got better. As we stood on the sidelines talking to several of the players parents my one-year old decided to pick that moment to take her first steps! (I really think she wanted to play!) I was so proud and happy to share my memories with my family that day in September and will continue to celebrate the success of the team - GO WILKES!

Molly age 3, Nora age 1 and Susan Dalton

Lehman and Compton Named to NSCAA All-Region Team

Two members of the Wilkes University women's soccer team have been honored by the National Soccer Coaches Association of America with berths on the Mid Atlantic All-Region team. Sophomore defender Dana Lehman (Redland/York Haven, PA) earned a spot on the second team, while senior forward Jennifer Compton (Oneonta/Oneonta, NY) was selected to third team.

Both players were instrumental in helping the Lady Colonels fashion an overall record of 15-4-1 this season. The duo also led Wilkes to their first Freedom Conference championship and the squad's first NCAA

Division III Tournament appearance.

"Dana is a very talented athlete and soccer player and this is well deserved recognition for her," commented Wilkes head coach John Sumoski. "We look forward to her contributions during the next two years. Jen has been here since my first year and has been a vital part of creating the culture that we have within our team. I'm extremely happy for her, especially since she was injured for half of her sophomore and junior seasons."

Lehman played a major role in helping Wilkes limit the opposition to just 1.07 goals per match this season. A first team All-Freedom Conference selection during both the 2004 and 2005 seasons, Lehman was instrumental in the Lady Colonels allowing an average of only nine shots per game. She was also a key contributor to a defensive unit that posted nine shutout victories during the campaign and allowed more than two goals only twice during the season.

Compton enjoyed an outstanding season for the Lady Colonels and was previously named to the All-Freedom Conference first team. After spending her first three seasons as a defender for Wilkes, she made the transition to the forward position this season and responded by scoring eight goals and dishing out one assist. Compton was credited with the game-winning goal in seven of the Lady Colonels school-record 15 victories this season. One

of those game-winners came in the team's 1-0 win over Drew University in the conference title match.

2006 Game Schedule

September			
1, Fri	Eastern University		Away
6, Wed	Messiah College		Away
9, Sat	Lebanon Valley College		Away
12, Tue	Elmira College		Home
16, Sat	Moravian		Home
18, Mon	Stevens Institute of Technology		Home
21, Thu	King's College		Home
23, Sat	Susquehanna University		Home
26, Tue	Lycoming College		Away
30, Sat	DeSales University		Away
October			
4, Wed	Kean University		Away
7, Sat	Fairleigh Dickinson University		Away
10, Tue	College Misericordia		Home
14, Sat	Delaware Valley College		Home
18, Wed	The University of Scranton		Away
21, Sat	SUNY Cortland		Away
24, Tue	Centenary College		Home
28, Sat	Drew University		Home
November			
1, Wed	Conf. Semi's		TBA
4, Sat	Conf. Finals		TBA
8, Wed	NCAA's		TBA

In 2011, John and Ann Dalton generously took their immediate family, children, spouses and grandchildren to Ireland to celebrate their 50th wedding anniversary and to renew their vows at John's family chapel in Sligo. We all went except for Ella who was not quite two years old yet. She stayed with Grammy and Pepere St.Onge in New Hampshire where she apparently ate a lot of oatmeal!

It was a wonderful trip with much history to learn and amazing countryside to see. John has cousins there and we were able to spend some time with them and even went to an Irish football game—don't ask me about the rules, it seems like a cross between American football, soccer, rugby and who-knows-what else! But the local crowd was passionate and one of the distant Dalton cousins was playing his heart out for the home team!

Among the many memories of that trip are the ones that are distinctly related to Susan. She had been talking for many years prior about wanting to get a tattoo. She wasn't sure what she wanted, but she knew she wanted one. Well, to her, what better place to get one than Dublin?

She researched tattoo artists and establishments and scheduled an appointment for an evening of down time on the trip. We left Molly and Nora with the family and set off to find the place. Ever deeper into the blue-collar, manufacturing heart of Dublin we ventured until we found the studio on the second floor of a turn of the century store-front building. The first floor store was boarded up, closed, with old signs revealing it used to sell top hats and topcoats. Where were we?

Once we found it, the studio turned out to be well-lit and surprisingly modern. The needles looked sharp and clean to my layman's eyes and I knew no amount of protest would matter. She had not told me what the tattoo would be or where it was going. Here it is. Upper left butt cheek.

I can still vividly see little Ella showering with her Mother, pointing up at Susan's butt to her name, etched there together with her sisters', connected by the Celtic Knot, for all eternity. It is an image that never fails to make me smile.

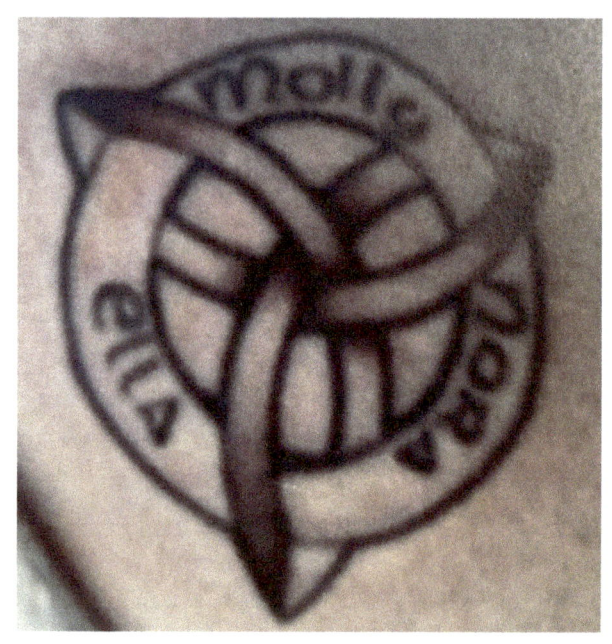

Chapter 13
Kick Donkey

By late spring, 2013, something was bothering Susan. Given what she had been through four years earlier following Ella's birth, and just how little she complained about her health, I knew it had to be something significant if she was mentioning it at all. Initially, she did not include me in her trip to her primary care physician, but when she was referred to oncologist Dr. Michael Wax, she wanted me there.

It was the dog days of summer and we were scheduled to head to New Hampshire for the traditional St.Onge family reunion on the first Saturday in August. Shortly before we were scheduled to go, Susan had several blood tests and a full work up. The test results would not be available until after the New Hampshire trip.

Atypical of her, she was very concerned with the test results pending. She chose not to join Molly, Nora and me on the drive. She opted to stay home with Ella which would begin a five-year practice of trying to keep things as normal as possible. She insisted that the girls be encouraged to continue to believe in unicorns, fairies and pixie dust for as long as possible, because real life would come for them all too soon. She insisted the older girls and I go and have fun.

That was easier said than done when a cancer diagnosis is hanging in the balance. I tried not to talk about it very much at the reunion. These things are supposed to be fun. And everybody has their challenges in life. A couple of my aunts, however, noticed that I was quieter than usual. I'm typically the guy who puts on his referee shirt and officiates the annual family water balloon toss with my whistle, rules and everything. (Well, the only rule is supposed to be "...thou shall not pelt thy referee with yonder water balloon." Way too many people in my family take far too much delight in breaking that rule.)

So anyway, one of my aunts who happened to be a nurse, coaxed my concerns out of me. When I told her that Susan was being screened for cancer, the response was, and I'm paraphrasing "oh, she's only 44 years old, she's too young and healthy to possibly get sick like that…"

Wouldn't that have been nice. Though my aunt meant well, she was sorely uninformed. I can't help but feel angry about the comment to this day.

I never repeated it to Susan because a week or so later she had her test results back.

I won't use these pages to discuss the formal diagnosis using all of the medical terminology. That's way above my pay grade. I will say, however, both Susan and her oncologist were optimistic. Stage two cancer. It was in the tissue in one breast and at least one lymph node.

Discussing her treatment options, there was no question in Susan's mind that she would have a double mastectomy and reconstructive surgery. Remember, this is a woman who had a breast reduction more than 20 years earlier so she knew what recovery would involve. She knew what she was signing up for. On top of that, she also chose, although it wasn't necessarily required at the time, to have a full hysterectomy. I'm sure there's a medical reason for it, but if memory serves, that step was optional. And she opted for it. She wanted to address all potential risk factors.

Oddly, there were several oncology appointments where I could tell that she and Dr. Wax were speaking in code, and/or they would simply ask me to step out of the room. Trusting both implicitly, I was obedient. It felt odd at times, but it was cancer after all. She wanted to talk to her doctor alone.

I certainly was not going to argue. For many people who know me, that last line may not seem to fit, but, well…time and place…

I will never forget the day that she made the decision to have the double mastectomy and the full hysterectomy at age 44. The look on her face was utter determination to survive.

She was not going to let cancer change her life. She wanted all infected tissue removed from her body... right then and there.

The first set of infusion days came and Susan embraced them with optimism and turned them into a celebration, in some respects. Each one was meaningful to her. As such, it was important to her to have different people join her at the infusion lab. Whether it was members of her Mom Crew, her parents, colleagues from work, she made a point to dress up nicely (albeit comfortably) and always made her day in the chair as much fun for her "guests" as for herself.

If you've ever been to an infusion lab you know that they can be sobering affairs. Some people are very private about their treatment. Some people have their headphones on and just do not want to be bothered.

While Susan respected other people's space, she was a traveling party unto herself! She made the atmosphere in those labs joyful. The nurses loved working with her. They often traded patients so they could spend time with her. She brought them coffee and flowers and always had some other type of trinket or baked goods for those patients seated around us. She made friends with several of them. I don't know what I expected, but that party atmosphere? Typical of Susan.

Front row, L to R - Jennifer Suwala Glander, Susan (she really didn't need the Wonder Woman apron!), Lori Bacon Fitzgerald. Back row, L to R - Tracy Stefanelli-Klurman, Patrice Connors Hanvey, Robin DeBrito, Stacey Conroy-Couzzo, Karen Tebben-Rossi, Pamela Jane Williams, Liz Sharp Higgins, Kathy Drivas, Terrine Chung Joe, Sharon Graham Solsky

Her treatment involved a varying cocktail of chemotherapy drugs. As one might expect, her hair started falling out in clumps in the shower and on her pillow. She decided to have "fun" with shaving it off. She and the girls dyed it pink and teased it out to a mohawk. We set up a stool in my basement shop and I shaved her head. With the kids watching, we both put on brave faces, but honestly, it sucked. I wound up having to do this twice—again when she was treated following remission.

In the days after an infusion, Susan was definitely not herself. Lethargic. Nauseous. A tinny-type taste in her mouth. She still answered the bell of Motherhood. Sure, we had to modify some of our routines in the house. The girls were still young. By 2014, Molly was 12, Nora was 10 and Ella was five. They were active. They had stuff to do. And so did Susan.

The bravest person I know, I also learned that she was probably the toughest. Following chemo she faced her surgeries head-on. And, she did it with a smile, or was it a smirk? I captured it in what I dubbed "Double Mastectomy Day 2014". Hair short for the first time in our life together…really short…we sat in the waiting room waiting for the surgeon. She was confident and determined. Look at the picture. Judge for yourself.

Double Mastectomy Day – 2014

Here is something they don't tell you in health class in high school, or when you're dating, starting a family, and thinking about spending your life with somebody. In preparation for her double mastectomy we had to sit down with a large three-ring-binder. We flipped through pages and pages of pictures as if we were looking at a police lineup. The thing was, it wasn't "perps" we were looking at. We were "nipple" shopping.

Yes. I said nipple.

It never occurred to either of us that her procedure included, potentially, replacing her nipples. At first, as you would expect from me and Susan, we had fun with it. We joked, we laughed. We giggled like school children.

About 30 minutes into it, however, Susan asked the logical questions, "How are they made? Where do they come from?"

I felt so bad for the poor physician assistant who was sitting with us. Her one word answer stopped Susan in her tracks.

"Cadavers."

Nope. Ever decisive, Susan closed the three-ring-binder and proclaimed there was no way she would do that. The PA then suggested she could have nipples "tattooed" on, completed with shading, depth and dimension. Susan replied, simply, "well, if I'm going to do that, I'm not going to waste tattoos on nipples... I'll put a four leaf clover on one, and a Fleur de Lis on the other." (She respected my French Canadian heritage and had been telling me to use the Fleur de Lis as my law firm's logo for years!)

Regrettably, Susan never got those tattoos.

While that was Susan's position regarding nipples from a cadaver, it was simply her personal preference. She would never have discouraged anyone from pursuing any form of healthcare or related matter if that's what they wanted for themselves. She was respectful that way. I know that Susan would support anyone's personal decision. The "nipple proposal," as it became known, just wasn't suitable for her.

What I did not know at that time, but learned the following year when I was doing our taxes, was that at least one of the reasons she and Dr. Wax asked me to step out of the treatment room occasionally was that they discussed the option of having a tummy tuck at the same time as the hysterectomy. I mean, it made sense, they would already be working in that same vicinity.

I can't remember if it was the same surgeon who did both the hysterectomy and the tummy tuck, but I was absolutely excluded from those meetings. I had no idea. I mentioned that I learned it while doing the taxes—the mastectomy and hysterectomy were partially covered by insurance but the tummy tuck was not.

Susan cashed out some of her IRAs to pay for that part of the procedure.

I had no idea! For the life of me, doing taxes in 2015, I could not figure out where an additional $15,000 of reportable and taxable income was coming from. It was the difference between a small refund and having to pay an additional amount of tax for that year. It was driving me crazy!

I did our taxes the entire time we were together, even through the law firm years. I took pride in being able to do it myself on TurboTax. But, I could not find where that extra income was coming from. After letting me vent and stew on it for a couple of days, she finally relented and told me what she had done.

It took me a while to understand the significance of it. She planned on surviving. And when she did, she wanted to look good. I mean, after three full-term pregnancies and the ravishes of chemo and surgeries, I thought she was still beautiful. But, self image, body image, self-esteem: I learned the hard way that you cannot argue with a woman over these things.

Moreover, how can you argue with somebody who wants to look good when they survive?

Conversely, if she didn't survive, the money wouldn't matter anyway. I guarantee, Spirit Susan still gets a chuckle about not telling me she closed out her IRAs.

The surgeries were largely successful. Recovery was tough on Susan, though. While she had experience with breast reduction from years earlier, I'm not sure if she was anticipating just how severe the recovery from the combination of all three at the same time—mastectomy, hysterectomy and tummy tuck—would be.

Unfortunately for Susan, I was her primary caregiver. As I've gotten older, I am finding that I am not good with blood and goop and icky stuff. She had six drainage ports attached in various places that needed to be emptied and cleaned multiple times throughout the day. Not going to lie, I probably should not have been on the top of the depth chart for that task!

We muscled through the post-surgery days with as much grace as we could. Susan would joke that she would probably have to put the worm on my hook if we went fishing. It's a good thing we didn't! But we soldiered through the tough stuff.

Recovery was slow but steady. And, in time, Susan's hair grew back. Her energy was restored, somewhat. So was her sense of humor. I'm not sure where she got it, but she loved a red T-shirt with a design on the front of a woman kicking a donkey. Of course, I couldn't understand why she would find that act of cruelty so endearing. She had to remind me what the other name for a donkey was so I would understand the imagery.

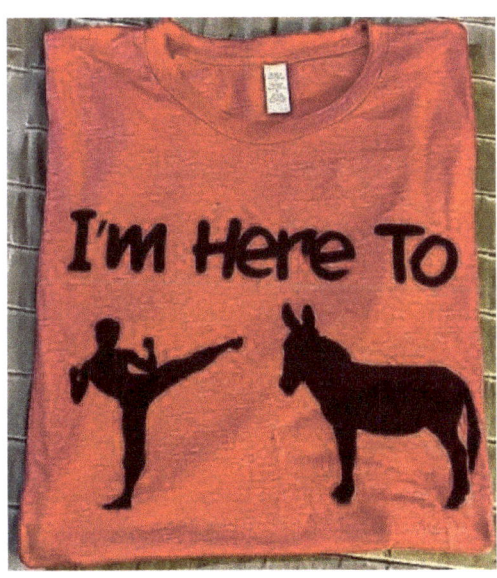

Following her full course of chemo and surgeries, Susan did, in fact, kick donkey. She kicked cancer into remission. Remission was largely kind to her with the singular exception that it was simply too short.

Regrettably there weren't many creature comforts that I was able to give Susan. Sure, we went on a few trips. We had the basics. But I never felt that I was able to truly give her the finer things in life. Not that she asked for them. But, I would've loved to have given her that gourmet kitchen I mentioned.

I'm very grateful that during her remission we were able to get her a decked-out Honda Odyssey. It was not her dream car, a convertible Mustang, but it had all the bells and whistles for family luxury! After years of long trips with substandard vehicles, she really wanted her kids to travel in style and comfort. Whether it was driving down the Garden State Parkway to Manasquan, or sitting in traffic in Connecticut on the way to New Hampshire, she wanted all the creature comforts for her family.

One of the things I was able to facilitate for her, through some of my work as an attorney, was to arrange a fairly sizable donation to her alma mater, Wilkes University. We worked very closely with then-Director of Alumni Giving (formerly the men's basketball coach) Jerry Rickrode. One of my clients had named me trustee of a sizable charitable trust and gave me discretion over a portion of those funds and where they could be donated. I asked Susan what she would do with the funds and she recommended Wilkes Women's Soccer. It resulted in the construction of a new women's soccer team locker room. Jerry and the folks at Wilkes did a wonderful job recognizing Susan. They invited her to campus to speak to the team before a game and Susan was bursting with pride at that opportunity.

In the first few years following Susan's passing, Jerry and the women's soccer program invited me, our daughters, and Susan's parents to one of their home games late in October in honor of Susan. Ella was probably 10 years old when she came with me one time and the women on the team took her out on the field during warm-ups. She had a blast! To this day, I continue to be friends with Jerry Rickrode and consider Wilkes an integral part of Susan's life. Even though we lived about two hours away, Susan loved going back for alumni events. She stayed connected to many in her friend group from that period.

Chapter 14
3:00 AM - June 21, 2018

18 months after kicking cancer, a regularly scheduled blood test revealed that it was back.

I am not sure I was ever told where "it was back," but it had progressed to stage four and I later learned that it spread to her midsection and the various organs there. Surgery was not an option. We would have to put our hopes in various chemotherapy treatments.

Back to the infusion lab. This time, no fanfare. Very few visitors were allowed. Relapse became a private thing, very unlike Susan.

During the first go-round with chemo I think we both believed, unconditionally, that she would survive. During her relapse, I still held that belief, or perhaps naiveté? Susan was far more concerned but other than wanting to keep her treatment private, she never revealed to me just how worried she was. Even during the very final days I think we both believed a miracle was possible.

By May-ish, 2018, Susan was on Doxil to fight her cancer. I only remember the name of that particular drug because I was also told that its nickname was "the red devil." Succinctly, Doxil was kicking HER donkey. She was losing weight, constantly nauseous and could not regulate her gastrointestinal functions.

During that time, I was running my law firm and developing a side hustle as a basketball referee. During the week of June 4, I was trying out to become a college official at a camp at a small college in New Jersey close to home.

Looking back on it now, I am very angry with myself. I think I suffered from the "frozen fish/frog" principle: the notion that you can so slowly and imperceptibly decrease the temperature surrounding a fish or a frog to the point where they actually freeze into suspended hibernation. I was the fish or frog being frozen. The changes were so slow, almost imperceptible over time, as we came to accept her new physical reality. The changes went almost unnoticed to me. Maybe I just didn't want to notice. Maybe Susan was great at concealing how she was really doing.

In any event, in late May and early June, she had a couple of really bad days that put her in the hospital for dehydration. She received treatment and IV fluids and was released. On or about June 7, however, I was scheduled to go back for a second or third night of the basketball camp when Susan told me, in our living room, that she needed to go to the hospital immediately.

There was no debate or discussion. From that moment on, I was on auto-pilot. There are huge gaps of time during the ensuing two weeks that I simply cannot remember. At the same time, there are incredibly minute details and occurrences for which I have no earthly reason to recall as clearly as I do. We called an ambulance and made arrangements for the girls. Her condition had deteriorated quickly. It was the last day she would be in our home.

I wanted to post updates of her condition on Facebook and request prayers. She did not want me to do so. I struggled with that. I believe in the power of prayer. I believe she did too, but her sense of privacy was also very strong.

Candidly, I have never been able to fully understand why she didn't want me to solicit prayers for her. There came a time, however, when I posted on Facebook anyway. The outpouring of support was significant, moving and heart-felt. It didn't help. My Susan was slipping away. Adding to that reality, she was mad at me when she found out I posted! Ugh!

Because I was on auto-pilot during that period, writing the rest of this chapter with any kind of coherence is virtually impossible. Or maybe I just don't want to.

That said, I hope the following gives you a sense of the chaos, confusion, focus, fear, assertive advocacy, disappointment, setback, hope, conviction, grace, dignity and reluctant acceptance that was her/our final days.

Grammar and syntax be damned, honestly, this is the best I can do.

June 7 – June 16, 2018

Taken by ambulance to the hospital, admission, delay, noise, confusion, days, nights, noise, constant nurse visits, no peace, multiple inconclusive tests, MRIs, heat, noise, bright lights, poor A/C, constipation, prune juice, treating symptoms but not the underlying cancer, keeping family informed, family meetings, long conversations, can't remember the topics, visitors, too many people, please stop, we need help, we need peace, noise, light, please stop the nurses from coming in so often, why is it sooooo hot, noisy, prune juice, tests, frail, labored breathing, pain, constant pain, make it stop, are we really talking about urns, I can't read my notes of what you want, I am so sorry, what can I do, I love you, I love you too….why won't the nurses stop, I finally just fell asleep, what do we tell the girls, when, too many well-meaning and well-intended voices that were NOT Susan's…

June 16, 2018

Saturday—constant interruptions, no rest, decision to seek peace in hospice, Father's Day the next day, fighting for release on a holiday weekend, arrange hospice, fight for transport and admission on a holiday, call to Dr. Wax late on a Saturday, unexpected reaction "she's finally accepted it…" heavy exhalation, Kevin shocked by his response, Susan's Father arranged Last Rites for Susan, administered at the hospital, Priest was pressed for time, had another event, gee, how do I rush a dying person, Last Rites? Really? Not sure what to think about that, still had hope, however naive it was…noise, lights, more nurse visits, make it stop….

June 17, 2018

Sunday, Father's Day—Kevin advocates, pushes hard for transfer to The Center for Hope Hospice, met my parents and the girls at a park mid-day for lunch and to play on the swing, wanted to tell them, but say what? Protecting them, hopeful, scared, barely keeping it together while Susan suffered, late Sunday evening, finally get all clearances for release, she just wants quiet, cool, A/C that works and no more nurse visits, assholes at the end, intentionally over-visiting, driving both of us crazy, did I mention they were assholes for what they did—actually barging into the room every 20 minutes and accomplishing nothing, nothing they did helped anything, we believed it was intended to compel Susan to leave the facility. Glad to be getting out of this EFFING hospital. Following the ambulance, took a picture with my phone following the ambulance, driving through Scotch Plains and Fanwood, past our neighborhood, past our home, to the hospice center…

Enter the quiet of hospice, the peace, the cool, the quiet, they gave us two rooms, I put some of our stuff in the other room but I slept at her side—we both finally slept!

June 18, 2018

Monday—gaining strength, believed she would get rest and recover and beat the odds and be among the precious few who walk out of hospice, Susan's pain medicine button, "beam me up Scotty," family visits, optimism…

June 19, 2018

Tuesday—too many family and friends visiting, no peace, minutes felt like hours, hours felt like seconds, making arrangements with counselors for the kids, anticipating the worst, Kevin doing this but not believing it was necessary—intellectually knew it was possible but emotionally naive—still believed Susan would walk out of hospice...

June 20, 2018

Wednesday—Susan wants to be alone with me, see her girls and just be...

Late day, cousin Rebecca flies in from her Martha's Vineyard vacation, John and Ann don't want her to stay with them, offered her a bed at our home, she sort of insists on staying in the second room we had in the hospice center—I should have insisted she leave or stay in that room—I didn't. I resent the whole situation because I wanted to be alone with Susan if/when she passed. Grudging acceptance that stress reveals character. I needed to be stronger in the face of that. I was being who I was—advocating for my Love and being present with her—trying in vain to protect her Spiritual peace in her final moments...

June 21, 2018

Thursday, approximately 2:00 AM—all family and friends gone except Rebecca—Susan has seen our girls for the final time (each had some time with her but still did not know that Mommy might actually die) the hospice center settles into its overnight "hum" — just the noise of some fluorescent lights and the soft murmuring of muted televisions—exhaustion, weakness, labored breathing, semi-consciousness, wearing out the pain medicine button, two chairs drawn up on either side of Susan to her knees, Rebecca doing breathing exercises or other quiet activity to center herself and be present, I wanted to ask her to go into the other room, but didn't. Couldn't. My hand resting on Susan's knee, my head on the bed next to it, so uncomfortable but it was the best I could do, I needed to touch her, to feel her, I needed her to feel me. I wanted to be awake for her in case she needed anything. I wanted to be of service to her.

I fell asleep.

3:00 AM—Rebecca heard Susan take her last breath, then went and got the duty nurse who confirmed the time of death (while I was sleeping at her knee) then the nurse woke me at 3:15 AM to tell me. The immediate cause of death on the certificate is "Metastatic Breast Cancer."

In short order, the Dooley Colonial Funeral Home was there to pick up Susan's body and transport her to their facility. The last time I saw her, Susan was in the hospice bed, neck and shoulders slightly elevated, lying on her back, head tilted to her right in the direction where I was sitting.... her hand reaching out, I want to believe as if to me. I do not have a photo of this. Don't need one. It is burned indelibly on my mind. Someday, I hope to dream that my hand reaches back to hers and we touch—again, and never let go.

For now though, no more labored breaths.

No more pain.

No more cancer.

No more Susan.

Her body was limp and lifeless, so very unlike Susan.

There was nothing there. There was no presence.

My larger than life Love was gone.

I couldn't feel her anymore.

I cried.

Sometimes my eyes feel as if I have never stopped.

I have not been able to sleep through the night of June 20 into June 21 since. Instead, I post a remembrance of her at precisely 3:00 AM so that our Facebook universe will be reminded of who and what we lost at that moment.

Chapter 15
Stories I Learned From Friends After She Passed

She was a messenger of hope and compassion. During Susan's Celebration of Life, I shared the following stories I received from people on Facebook or in other messages.

Nic Tremblay

Nic: Years ago, when we were all younger, I found myself at a family wedding. Being a shy and painfully awkward kid, this wasn't a place that I thrived. So, once the dancing and festivities began I sat in a chair and endured the passing minutes that turned to hours, just waiting to get a respite from this "socializing" thing that I couldn't seem to get a grasp on.

Enter Susan. Sensing my turmoil she invited me to the dance floor for an impromptu lesson. It was under the guise of dance but, in actuality, it was a lesson in kindness and how putting such kindness into motion, even as simple an act as a "dance lesson," can go a long way towards elevating those in need.

This was years ago but the memory is vivid. Her smile was bright and, thinking back, I'm still amazed at the ease and grace she demonstrated while delivering a simple, but much needed, lesson in kindness. The beauty she spread will ripple through the lives of all who knew her. Myself included.

Meg B.

Meg: Kevin, I'm so sorry. Susan was so kind to me at the Marist senior formal—I may have been over served (read drunk) and she held my hair while I threw up. I had just met her. Stay strong and her memory will live on in your beautiful, strong, courageous girls.

Melissa Carsillo

Melissa: Hi Kevin, my mother worked with Sue at FDU. I was also a student at that time. I'm in shock to hear of her passing. She was a wonderful person. I will keep you all in my thoughts and prayers during this most difficult time.

KMS Response: Thank you. My sincerest hope is that people who knew her stay in touch with our daughters so that they are constantly reinforced with the memory of their Mother.

Melissa: That is easy to do. She saw something in me that no one else saw. She gave me my interview and accepted me into FDU. For me this was a "reach school." My learning disability made it hard for me to get good grades but Sue offered the interview and with that one interview I was able to succeed through four years of college as well as get my master's degree. I just completed my 15th year of teaching at the elementary level. I'm not sure where I would be without that one small gesture by your wife. I'm sorry I wasn't able to thank her more for that opportunity.

Stephan Kolodiy

Stephan: Hi Kevin, I never met you but I just wanted to drop a line to say how sorry I am for your loss. Susan was my boss at Stevens and I will never forget her. I was 27 years old at the time and was diagnosed with testicular cancer. I remember sitting in Susan's office right after I found out. I was crying and she was incredibly supportive and empathetic. I had no idea that she relapsed and I'm sorry that I never took the time to see her after I left Stevens. This world certainly lost a great one. My condolences to you and your family.

So many people have shared their own Susan Stories with me over the years. Although I did not know some of them at the time of her

Celebration of Life, these stories keep coming and continue to warm my heart. Following are a few.

<u>*Dina Gavenas*</u>

It's so ironic to have heard from Kevin. I have recently experienced some big life changes —divorce, multiple moves, managing two teenagers and two dogs while working 7 days a week. One of the moves brought me to Sue's old neighborhood and I found myself thinking about her often. I knew if she were still here, she would show me and the kids around, tell us where all the good restaurants were and make sure we knew where all the fun places were. I know in my heart that, although time would have passed, she would have embraced my family with hers.

I also found myself thinking about her when I passed the Hope House where Sue took her last breath, and I had the honor and privilege of getting to say goodbye, thanks to Kevin.

He had tried to get me in to see Sue when she was still in the hospital, understandably Sue just wanted privacy. I gave him an old key I had that I kept close, it had the word "Faith" stamped on it. He gave it to her, and seeing it around her neck when she passed let me feel like she knew I was there trying to help in some small way.

Sue and I met as freshman in college and were each thrilled to connect with a fellow Jersey Girl. We were different for sure. Sue was adventurous, peppy and always up for the next big excursion. She never really seemed to let things get to her, always footloose and fancy free. I was more serious, had to constantly hit the books to make it in the nursing program, and had to work a lot to afford being there. I found myself resentful of Sue sometimes, if I'm being honest, because she didn't seem to ever really worry...lol.... about anything. But, the older and wiser me now sits back and appreciates that we all need to channel our inner "Sue" ... and not take life so seriously all the time. I think about that lesson often-and will try to carry it with me always, like my memory of Sue. ❤️

Halloween 1988
Susan dressed up as Dina wearing her nursing pinafore
Dina dressed as Susan wearing her soccer uniform 😊

♥♥♥♥♥♥♥♥♥♥♥♥♥♥♥♥♥♥♥♥♥♥♥♥♥♥♥♥♥♥♥♥♥♥♥♥

Mark Sapara

When I first returned to FDU in November 2001, almost everyone I met (and those I already knew) told me that I had to meet someone named Susan St.Onge. I found it notable that almost everyone who met me said the same thing! Their vibe was that Susan and I were "one in the same" and would get along famously!

So, on my first day at the Teaneck campus, I found my way to my new office in Dickinson Hall to find out that Susan, who worked in Advancement, was just upstairs. So, I almost

119

immediately make my way up to the 4th floor, walk into the Advancement Office, and there she is. I walk up to her, introduce myself, and tell her the story I've been told about "us." With that gorgeous wide smile of hers, Susan grabs me and gives me the biggest hug and tells me that we are newfound friends.

And so it began. It's hard to enumerate every story about Susan that I have in the 17 years I knew her. But there are a few memories that illuminate me whenever I get sad about her passing. One of the best (and funniest!) was the night of the FDU Charter Day gala in June 2002. I originally wasn't intending to go, but somehow I got a ticket (maybe even through Susan) and a couple of colleagues figured out a way to wrangle a tuxedo for me, fitted and all, within a couple hours' notice of the event.

Earlier in the day, I had been talking to Susan about how I was looking to buy a house I had seen online. She was adamant that she be the first person I tell about its outcome. So while I'm simultaneously mulling over the biggest purchase of my life, I'm trying to finagle a last minute invite to the Great Gatsby-ish event that was taking place that same evening.

It turns out that I got cold feet and decided not to make the purchase. Knowing I was going to see Susan that night at Charter Day, I figured I'd wait to tell her, mindful that she would be the FIRST person who knew. That evening, I showed up to Charter Day, immediately searching for Susan. I saw her across the lawn (she was maybe 7 or 8 months pregnant with Molly, so she wasn't hard to find!). She was surrounded by people (as she always was!) and I ran up the group, energetic and gasping and just blurted out, "Susan, I didn't do it!"

The crowd goes quiet, Susan looks at me, points down to her pregnant stomach, and starts to giggle. In realizing that these folks had NO idea what was going on, and that a joke was looming in the air, I shouted while pointing at her stomach, "And if you say

I did, I will deny it!" The group just cracked up and we all laughed in what pretty much was a belly-aching guffaw.

That entire night, I followed Susan around, patting her stomach and saying "Seriously, I didn't do it!" And that was how Susan was, almost every day of our friendship. Someone with whom I had few boundaries, endless laughter, thoughtful and deep talks, and a friendship that everyone knew would blossom and one that I never expected.

The stories like that are numerous. Every time I think of her, these images come to mind, whether it was making a crank-call with her from the Landmark restaurant in Livingston, to times at the shore house with "the girls," to pizza nights in Fanwood as each of her three daughters came into this world and flourished under her care.

Mark and Susan
FDU Charter Day 2004

♥♥♥♥♥♥♥♥♥♥♥♥♥♥♥♥♥♥♥♥♥♥♥♥♥♥♥♥♥♥♥♥♥♥♥♥♥♥

Jennifer Russell Yearwood

I met Susan St.Onge when she moved to Badger Street in Concord NH in the mid-1990s. Her presence was like the most perfect sunny warm summer day in NH; you just felt good being around her and didn't want the time together to end. She instantly made life more fun, and I looked forward to seeing her and spending time with her.

I was trudging my way through high school with a subpar boyfriend that I thought was the best I could do, and Susan helped shine the light on the inside of me. Without telling me he was worthless, she helped me see how worthwhile I was. She was a big sister and confidant that didn't judge or make you feel silly, and I needed that kind of support in my high school years.

I remember her teaching me all the ropes about driving a stick shift as we'd travel back and forth to Manchester to go shopping on many occasions. I was just learning to drive at the time. We'd jam out to Duran Duran, and she'd recite all the words. She even helped me pick out one of my high school formal dresses and made it the most special experience I could have asked for.

Susan's partner in life and soul mate was Kevin, and he was a wonderful example of a husband whenever we'd interact. I learned about Marist College through their love story and when I went to visit the college my senior year in high school, I fell in love with Marist and went there too!

I lost touch with Susan through the years after I got married and she had her 2nd child, Nora, but her impact on my life was unforgettable in the most enchanting way. I am a better person because Susan St.Onge was in my life.

(L-R) Kevin and Jen, Susan and Jen

♥♥♥♥♥♥♥♥♥♥♥♥♥♥♥♥♥♥♥♥♥♥♥♥♥♥♥♥♥♥♥♥♥♥♥♥♥

Amanda Fossett Hosmer

I've heard people say a single person can change your life in an instant, and I believe it because that was what happened to me the day I met Susan Dalton St.Onge.

Susan's husband & partner in crime, is Kevin. Kevin and my now husband, Terry, were suite mates, volleyball teammates. They are friends to this day. Terry had met Susan through Kevin and really wanted me to meet them. We were still dating, so this was probably around 1996. I was nervous meeting his friends, wanting to make a good impression, feeling a bit awkward etc. Terry assured me we'd all hit off.

We arrived at Susan's parents' house in Manasquan, New Jersey and what happened next I remember like it was yesterday. I was barely out of the car and here comes Susan—literally bounding out of the house, arms wide open and that light-up-her-face $1000 smile. She pulled me into a hug and said "I've heard so much about you and we're going to be great friends."

As easy as that, we did indeed become great friends! There was nothing superficial about our friendship and it will always be one of the most important relationships in my life. We found out we had a lot in common—food-likes, music, clothing, things we did and even a weird little bump we both had in the same place in our mouths where we constantly bite.

Susan was confident, spontaneous, could always bring a smile, knew when to listen and when to give advice. She was understanding and accepting. All of this later in life would make her a wonderful Mom too. Susan pushed me out of my comfort zone and helped me be more confident in myself. How could you not be friends with such a person?

Over the years we shared so many good times together, with our husbands, other friends and families. There was a lot of laughter but we were also able to share the tears and hard times too. We shared many milestones and along the way we became more like family.

Susan had a way of making everything special, fun or an adventure. I remember a time the 4 of us were visiting in New Hampshire and decided to go to breakfast on the way to driving up the Mt. Washington Auto Road. EVERY place we stopped at along the way was either closed, had an event or had a 2 hour wait. Rather than get upset or frustrated, Susan just laughed at each stop and said "our quest continues!" It became a game. We finally ended up at an Applebee's around 1:00 PM. With her, it was never about the destination, it was about the journey, the laughs, friendship and memories of that day. Mt. Washington was pretty amazing, but, my favorite part of the day was getting there.

I feel so very honored to have known her, shared her story and that she wanted to be a part of mine. It was a privilege seeing her become a Mom to Molly, Nora and Ella. She told me once that she was nervous about being a Mom, but she was a natural and to this day she loves and cares for those 3 beautiful girls.

I hold close all my memories with Susan. She put herself out in the world and lived life her way—just not long enough. I often think "what would Susan say or do?" … She will always be a part of me and who I am.

Dammit—I miss her something terrible 🧡

Me, Susan, Amy and Terry Hosmer
atop Mount Washington

♥♥♥♥♥♥♥♥♥♥♥♥♥♥♥♥♥♥♥♥♥♥♥♥♥♥♥♥♥♥♥♥♥♥♥♥♥

Alisa Tagliareni Wasserman

Dear Molly, Nora and Ella:

I was honored when your Dad reached out to me, mentioning that he was writing a memoir about your Mom and asked if I would like to contribute … how can I say no!

I am sure you have all heard this before, but that is because it was so damn true—Susan would light up a room! So warm, friendly and funny! People would meet her and want to be friends with her because she had such a way of making you feel important, valued and heard … so sincere.

Your Mom was a dancer and very proud of her talent. She held herself with confidence, respect and a "don't mess with me" attitude! (well….she would use a different word than "mess" — Hee, hee!).

Family was a priority in her life and she loved you girls so much and worried about your well-being (as all Moms do!). Her face would light up when she saw one of you or talked about you. Even though some days can be tough for Moms, she was so patient and calm.

Memories I have of Suziwan (my nickname for her) all revolve around having fun, having meaningful girl talks, and going for joy rides (she drove, of course) whether to McDonald's or through the Watchung Reservation (at night with the headlights off—but JUST for a second)..or just to nowhere…these fun times created adventures and your Mom was very adventurous! Always game to try something new and interesting… she was never dull or boring.

She would get this little twinkle in her eye and a smirk when she was thinking of doing something a little outlandish…and was always able to convince you to join her…and afterward, you were glad you did!

126

Pink was her favorite color and she loved her pink cowboy boots! She was always cracking her knuckles and was a HUGE fan of Duran Duran!

In my eyes, your Mom was a strong, independent, fun and sincere woman. You each have something of your Mom's— whether it be a mannerism, a look, a like or dislike—embrace them, for, even though Mom is not here with you, she is still with you, but in a different way... inside your mind, heart and soul. No one can take that away from you. I am a big believer that you will see her again one day ... you will see her soul and you will know it is her immediately because she is your Mom.

Love you all and please know, I am always here for you...no matter when, no matter what...

Alisa and Susan

♥♥♥♥♥♥♥♥♥♥♥♥♥♥♥♥♥♥♥♥♥♥♥♥♥♥♥♥♥♥♥♥♥♥♥♥

Kevin invited me to share a memory or story of Sue. Isolating only one memory or only one story of Sue is near impossible when she is woven into the fabric of my being. Considering Sue's nickname for me was "Cheese" because of how sentimental I am, this may be longer. I will also try to keep my memories or stories on the low-end of the "hanky scale." (Sue and I used to rate movies, such as "Beaches" or "Steel Magnolias," based on the number of hankies we would go through. Sue would say there was the normal score, then my score—which was 10x's as much as the normal score because I would cry 10x's more.)

I first met Sue in January of our 7th grade years at Westfield's Edison Junior High School. I just moved to Westfield from Cranford after my parents divorced and my family home was sold. Sue and I were not extremely close in middle school because of my personal circumstances, but I felt at ease with her and gained a sense of belonging in my new environment when in her presence. I'm sure you have heard this repeatedly: Sue's smile and laugh were inviting and contagious and one would instantly feel her warmth and genuineness. We had some classes together, but we really got to know each other through the Duran Duran "clique," which included Sue, Karen Dahlinger, Jennifer Morrotta and Colleen Shea. We would fawn over their latest videos, posters and songs.

We had our own interests in high school. We had our own obligations. For me, working and seeing my Dad on the weekends; for Sue, it was Saturday football games with the marching band and band tournaments, soccer games and the beach house during the Summer. And, we each had our own goals.

Throughout high school, our friendship circles were closely interconnected: I spent most of my time with Karen Dahlinger, and Lisa and Angela Henry. Sue spent most of her time with Alisa and Sue. We would almost always come together for innocent—and I do mean, innocent—silly, stomach-hurting-from-laughter fun. We were a rare group of high school students who still knew how to play. We didn't need drugs or alcohol; we just needed each other's company for a great time. Our gift to one another was non-judgemental laughing with—and, yes, at times, at—one another about any subject of life, which gave each of us the greatest gift of being our true, authentic selves. When we laughed at each other, it was never malicious or cruel. It was usually a veiled lesson on laughing at oneself—because life is funny. There was no pretension, no airs. We could be as bold and brave, yet vulnerable—and as silly, goofy, dreamy and whimsical, yet soulful and serious—as we wanted or needed to be. The bonds of our friendships were real, honest and pure.

It is difficult to isolate high school memories with Sue. I do remember one night playing a pretend game of baseball behind Roosevelt Junior High School. One of us called the plays ("she hit a double…"), while the rest of us pretended to field the ball. This memory is vivid not only because we were having fun, just laughing and playing, but also because at one point Sue yelled from the darkness, "Avoid second base! I just peed all over it!"

During our college years, we had our share of pricey long distance phone bills as we periodically checked-in with each other. On breaks, we would immediately meet up in Westfield and easily pick up where we left off with our laughing and playing. I always felt comfort knowing I could exhale, relax and be myself around Sue.

At my graduation party, Sue broke the news that not only had she met a guy (yes, Kevin), but she needed to take one more class and complete her student teaching. Come Fall, I would be on my own.

I started work as a paralegal, which, again not to mince words—sucked. When Sue finished her obligations, she joined me at the law offices. This is when she and I really began to laugh and play. Once Alisa graduated and (finally) Sue Letwink, we had each other as we navigated our post-college, early-20's years which allowed us to be selfish and care-free—one of the very few times in life when you can be: You're not married. You don't have children. You are finding yourself in your career, in life and in relationships. We all eventually found ourselves in our careers, our relationships and marriages, but most importantly, in motherhood.

I'm going to pause here to explain the word "finally" when it comes to Sue Letwink. When Sue Letwink turned 21, I exclaimed "Finally!" because we no longer had to sneak her into bars or dance clubs. First Sue and I would go in. Then Sue would give me her ID. I would "forget something in the car," leave and give Sue's ID to Sue Letwink who was patiently waiting.

The four of us continued to play. We enjoyed tiramisu and cappuccinos at the coffee shop. We would watch 90210 and Melrose Place faithfully with each other, each week. We would go dancing and to concerts. We would make dinners together or go to dinner together.

Three pages in and I am just getting to memories, stories and observations:

Although I always think of Sue as brilliant and smart, school was hard for her. She was very quick and witty, though. You would greet her with, "What's up?" and her response would be, "Not my IQ!" or "Not my bra size!" You would leave saying, 'Well, I'm off." And her response would be, "...like a prom dress in the backseat."

Sue's humor was disarming and effortlessly hilarious. A person once said to me that Sue could always find the silver lining. Yes, she could with her optimism and smile. But more importantly, Sue had the unique ability to find humor in life. Life was very funny and fun for her. She embraced and embodied it.

I remember Sue once calling my house and my mom answered:

Sue: "Hi, Mrs. McCord. I mean, Bartram."

My mom: "Sue, you're old enough now. You can call me Jane."

Sue: "Well then, you can call me Miss Dalton."

Before my first date with Tom, I called Sue. I was feeling tired of relationships. Sue knew Tom from high school and knew he was a good guy. She said, "Laura, you're single and you hate to cook. At least go for the free meal." And so I went. 25 years of marriage and two children later, "free meals" are still discussed in our house. In fact, when Tom and I purchased our wedding bands, we brought them to separate jewelers for engraving. After our wedding ceremony on the way to our reception, Tom and I took them off and found we had both inscribed "free meals" in the other's wedding bands.

Sue and I had a falling-out in August 2001. On that night, I discovered a stone had fallen out of my wedding band. Later that night, I learned I not only lost a stone, but I lost my friend. The stone was replaced, but never the same. The friendship would never be the same and could never be replaced.

I last hugged Sue at the funeral of a good friend of ours. Sue and Kevin sat directly in front of me in the church. Even though twelve years had passed since our falling-out, the awkwardness was palpable. During the sign of peace, I knew I needed to reach out to Sue, if for no one else, it was for our friend who had passed away. Friendships meant the world to him. I tapped Sue on the shoulder and we embraced. Our hug was long and emotional and healing. The date was June 21, 2013. Five years to the day later, Sue left earth.

In June 2018, I noticed the stone in my wedding band was missing again. The next day, Sue Letwink called me to inform me Sue entered hospice. Weeks later, I had the empty spot in my ring filled with gold rather than replacing the stone. The gold-fill permanently memorializes our friendship in my wedding band.

I think of Sue daily. As I wrote in the beginning, she is woven into the fabric of my being and remains—and will always remain—a large presence in my life. When I'm confronted with a hardship, I think, "What would Sue do?" She would find and embrace the humor.

When people who never met Sue ask me to describe her, my best response is: Sue is the epitome of the phrase "larger than life." Sue's impact on this world is truly larger than her all-too-short time on this earth.

♥♥♥♥♥♥♥♥♥♥♥♥♥♥♥♥♥♥♥♥♥♥♥♥♥♥♥♥♥♥♥♥♥♥♥♥♥

Sue Sabol

I had the pleasure of being introduced to Susan back in the late 1990's through a mutual friend. At the time, she was working at FDU and not feeling fulfilled in her role and her manager was driving her a bit nutty. One evening when a bunch of us were having some post work tasty cocktails, I had mentioned to Susan that I needed to expand my work team and right away she said "oh I'd love to work for you. I don't know your field but I need to get out of this work environment I'm in." Instantly I said "yes, let's do it! Come work for me. I'll train you on the role—no problem. I need enthusiastic, smart and friendly people—and you fit it perfectly. Let's do it, Susan." She was overjoyed with the new opportunity.

What a stellar employee and friend Susan was. She took on her new role with such courage, energy, dedication and one hell of an amazing smile. Susan enthralled her co-workers, me included. She was quickly on her path to success. I loved her ideas for the role, her presentation style was one with such poise, her tenacity of fulfilling each task with such quality was wonderful. The one thing that I gained the most admiration for/of Susan was her friendly and caring way.

She and I became more than just work colleagues, we were girlfriends. Sharing stories of our lives, listening with keen ears and giving each other the support we needed to hold each other up when needed. We quickly became known in the office as "The Sue's"—we loved it. Our circles became so entwined that within a few months our office needed to create a distinction—so The Sue's became Sue O. and Sue S. We loved it!

The delight of she and Kevin expecting their first baby was seen in her everyday. But one thing she couldn't see, as the pregnancy weeks increased, were her feet! She swelled up so badly, she hated taking on more steps than her work day required. The swelling got so bad that one day she came to work all pretty in her dress with flip flops on in the middle of our NJ winter! We all felt for her. She claimed to be embarrassed of her new daily work look that would continue as baby Molly was growing. We all were like heck no...take that baby of yours and show off the pride of motherhood and embrace the ups and downs it'll be from this point on.

That's exactly what Susan did. She took a ton of pride in being a mother. Her life was fulfilled with her new role and title of Mommy. Nothing fit her finer for the remainder of her days on earth. Her smile will always be contagious, her friendship always enduring.

Thanks Sue O. for the years of friendship, laughter and being so amazing!

I miss you being here.

With love,

Sue S.

♥♥♥♥♥♥♥♥♥♥♥♥♥♥♥♥♥♥♥♥♥♥♥♥♥♥♥♥♥♥♥♥♥♥♥♥

Kerriann Broussard

Because I Can

When asked to write down a memory, I found myself struggling to identify that moment—that iconic, normal period of time that everyone will eventually recollect with detail that makes you feel like you've been there. Most of the stories will be about her sense of humor, her gracious time with friends and family, being an instinctual and real mom and endearing wife and daughter. I realized pretty quickly that I don't have those types of stories and that our friendship was neither neighborhood gal pal nor college dorm-life story-type.

We became friends through friends after college and our story was a distant one, with me being completely envious of the people that did have that type of relationship with her. I often found myself saying that if Sue and I were friends growing up or during college we would have been THAT dangerous duo which is probably why we connected so well. What I saw in Sue isn't a story or some cute anecdote. I saw a sister in crime that lived her life with humor in really "real" situations and she would have lived her future the same way. Because of her character, because of her drive, she is pushing me forward each and every day.

I have a home office like most people these days. I stare at past life artifacts, pins, gadgets and photos that keep me laughing. I also have two items that keep me grounded. The first artifact is Sue's memory card from her funeral. It's a photo of her raising a glass of wine to the person taking the photo with the capture of "A Drinking Song" by W.B. Yeats. Adorning this photo is a bracelet I wore during several years working a breast cancer event with the words, "The One I Miss" on it. This sits below the inevitable pins and trinkets and above a Mother's Day card that says, "You're Cool Beans." This photo makes me laugh because each and every time Sue and I were together with friends it was over a frozen concoction of some sort so I have to put words into her mouth at the time the photo was taken with her saying, "well, if I must adult today, let's have a glass of wine." However, secretly, I hear her voice saying, "ok Ker, how much ice do we need so that we don't feel guilty over the amount of tequila in here." Like I said, trouble twins.

The second artifact is a post-it note on the bottom left of my computer. It never leaves me while I'm working, traveling for work or in the office. It's a blue, well-protected note that says, "Because I can..." with Sue's name below it amongst two other people.

You're probably asking the not-so-obvious reason for these two items. When searching for my story about Sue, I realized that I couldn't be the girlfriend with some true horrid college or school day story. I can't be that person that tells the secretive neighborhood or vacation-type story that always has a funny ending with Sue involved. However, I did promise myself something after her funeral that I would gift her one last gift for the rest of my life—I would live my life the way she probably would, <u>because I can</u>, and I would like to believe that the life I strive to live every day is the one she would have lived. I can't say thank you to Sue for giving me those times we were hanging out, but, I can truly hear her saying, "get busy living sista."

I often find myself wondering what our relationship would be like years later. Inevitably I feel life would have gotten in the way with our families, we would have gotten together for a frozen glass of something or for food that we knew we shouldn't be eating (but what the hell) and told some humorous stories about our husbands that were playing golf and then it would turn into some unnerving conversations about sex and the male anatomy that were more humorous and true than embarrassing (not for us of course because "we're all perfect" we'd say and discuss our bra sizes) and more than likely we'd say we've got to do this more often because it's just too darn funny not to…and then we'd go our separate ways until the next time.

Until the next time.

Today, I stare at that photo while I work, pretending it's a frozen margarita and explain the blue post-it another several times to my coworkers who see it when we're together and I'm reminded, again, that "yes I can" and I can do it for you, Sue.

Sue, my gift to you, for giving me the gift of your true self, for not being afraid to be real, for the shared stories, for giving me a sense of girlfriend-hood when I didn't know I was even missing out on it, and for sharing a part of your life so genuinely each and every time we were together, is to live to be the person you would have been today—as a mom, wife, daughter and friend—while drinking a frozen concoction with too much tequila.

And I do this, because I can.

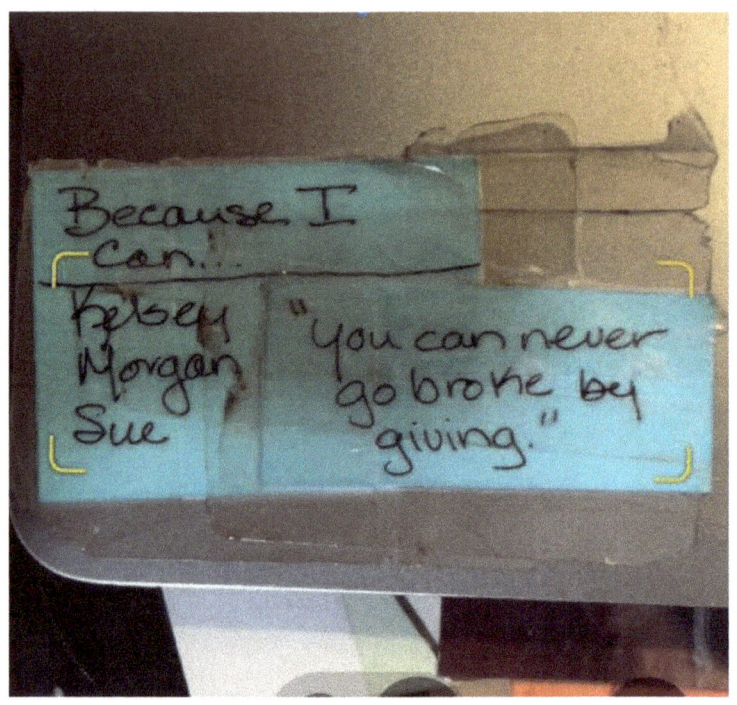

♥♥♥♥♥♥♥♥♥♥♥♥♥♥♥♥♥♥♥♥♥♥♥♥♥♥♥♥♥♥♥♥

Christine Chaillet

Before the age of cellphones, before the age of everyone having email, and long before the internet was the norm, I met Susan.

We had both gotten into Wilkes-Barre College and we were matched up to be roommates. I can't remember who, but I am sure it was Susan who reached out and wrote first. We exchanged letters and, no surprise, she sounded great. We decided to meet up and we met at a Wendy's. I knew immediately that I had struck gold.

My memory isn't what it used to be; for me, it was a turbulent time. So I don't remember moving into our dorm room. I can tell you that she took the right side of the room and I took the left. I can also tell you that in that short time, I was at Wilkes-Barre, we became fast friends. As with everyone who knew her, she made me laugh and feel special.

I only stayed at school for a few months. As mentioned, it was a turbulent time for me. I was suffering from depression and unresolved childhood trauma. I had to leave campus without a proper goodbye. I know that my leaving the way I did was not fair to her and probably caused her much stress. At the time, she was probably happy not to have a troubled roommate, but, with her heart of gold, I know she probably worried. Either way, she had a good story to tell of her crazy freshman roommate.

Time passes.

Years.

I often wondered what ever happened to Susan because as time would have it, I now lived in the same area I remembered that she grew up in. I wondered if our paths would ever pass... and then they did. One night, after having my third child, I was scrolling through Facebook and I received a Facebook notification of "you might know Susan."

Yes, I do! We had a mutual friend which is why Facebook recommended her to me. I wasn't sure what to do. Would she want to hear from the college roommate that left under such circumstances? What would I say? I decided to go ahead and send her a message through Facebook.

My message was very generic because I was uncertain if it was her and even if it was, I was uncertain if she would want to hear from me. I just sent a message stating who I was and how I thought I knew her. I then apologized for all the drama. Not surprising, her reply was perfect. She even commented that she couldn't drive past a Wendy's without thinking of me. We reconnected and even made a plan to meet up as we realized that we literally lived within walking distance.

We met-up to rehash the drama of my college exit. That could have been the end of it, but a new friendship was formed. We realized that we had kids in similar ages, that we both married "Kevin's" and that it was fun to hang out with each other.

As a final note to the sign of Susan's grace, whenever we were together and people asked how we knew each other she would simply say, "we were college roommates."

♥♥♥♥♥♥♥♥♥♥♥♥♥♥♥♥♥♥♥♥♥♥♥♥♥♥♥♥♥♥♥♥♥♥♥

Chapter 16
Stories I Learned From Family
After She Passed

<u>*Cousin Rebecca Shafer DeJesus*</u>

My Buddhaful Sister

I have so many memories of my cousin Susan. Trying to capture one of them and write about it in detail feels like trying to lasso a comet from a starry-skied night. My therapist tells me that there are still more layers to the grief. In reality, my world has recently only just begun to spin again upon its axis since losing her more than 6 years ago.

Thanks to trusty ole Facebook and its elusive algorithms, a memory popped up recently that made me weak in the knees.

January, 2015. Susan was well into her journey in the #F——cancer club. She brought the girls to see us at our home in Pennsylvania. I, myself, was just over two years into my journey of not being able to have kids of my own. Surgical onset menopause had my mind running circles around itself. The grief of that loss was attempting to swallow me whole, boots and all.

While the girls were in the living room, Susan noticed the enormously large Buddha head that was on display in our dining room. My brother, who knows of my love for all things steeped in Eastern traditions, had gifted it to us a few weeks prior for Christmas. Though I do actually really like it, admittedly it is too out-of-place for that small space, and I hadn't yet found its forever home in our house.

As I was rambling on about my sadness and anxiety and sleepless nights, Susan looked me square in the eyes and said, "We'll get through this! And I can share my girls with you!" Then she grabbed the Buddha head, positioned it in front of her face, and started talking to me in a mock-meditation-teacher way, saying, "Just breeaaaathe! It's all going to be okay! Master Buddha says you're going to be alright! We all love you Aunt Beckles!"

In a way, it's kinda one of those you-had-to-be-there moments to really appreciate the depth of how funny it really was. But if you were lucky enough to have ever been in Susan's presence, you needn't have been there to know exactly what I mean. Susan had the ability to bring levity to the heaviest of situations. She had a way of providing light in the darkest of nights. And here she was—facing an illness of her own that threatened her very existence—and she was cheering me on.

Susan always had this way of making you feel like you were the most important person in the room. She always made me feel like anything and everything was possible. The relationship I had with my own sister was rocky in recent years, and Susan easily stepped into that role, no permission needed. We had always been close as cousins. And as we both stepped out of the quarter-life phases of our own journeys and headed towards middle-age, we grew even closer. Her daughters became my nieces. Her triumphs bolstered my own self-esteem. And her struggles tugged at my own chordae tendineae.

I can only hope that I enlightened her life even a fraction of how much she did mine. I trust that I did my best to help her feel like the most important person in the room, at least once. And as I carry out the rest of my days, I will forever cherish how blessed I am to have had Susan in my life. And I am beyond grateful to still experience her spirit through Molly, Nora, Ella, and Kevin.

♥♥

Cousin Matthew Shafer

(Excerpted from Matthew Shafer's Facebook post, June 26, 2018)

"To everything there is a season, and a time. To every purpose under the heavens above: A time to be born, a time to die; a time to plant, and a time to pluck up that which is planted; A time to kill, and a time to heal; A time to break down, and a time to build up; A time to weep, and a time to laugh; and a time to mourn."

The world lost a very very special and unique one of a kind, once in a lifetime person, my sweet dear cousin Susan Dalton St.Onge; BUT at the same time the world learned a VERY critical lesson and was reminded that it is SO important to live and love every moment of every day and every person you share life with, to live life to the fullest and to have no regrets, no animosity, no hate, no anger, no negativity, no drama, no one-upmanship, just simple love of life and love of people, no agendas!

Susan, you exemplified such selfless qualities, your electric personality was unmatched, even by me! You were such a simply amazing person! I have always admired you, your strength, wisdom, parenting skills, and your composure. Your presence was always felt so deeply whenever you were around, and I am certain (actually I know) many will agree with all of this.

Heaven just received an Angel from earth. It is with my deepest sorrows that my cousin Susan, whom I have shared a lifetime of memories with, has just passed away. From the days of family gatherings when we were toddlers, opening Christmas gifts, rocking it out to Duran Duran and Culture Club in the attic as preteens, great times with our brothers and my sisters, to riding the infamous waterslide every summer over at Manasquan beach as teens, to the roots of the early days listening to U2's Boy, October, and War, and the many many years watching fireworks at Manasquan Beach with your folks my Aunt Ann and Uncle John, and then we added our kiddos over the last almost 15 years now, and running together with Team Freedom in the Spring Lake 5 every year.

My dear cousin, I am going to miss you dearly Susan. You left a remarkable impression on the world, much more than a legacy. Thank you for being such a role model to many.

Many people walk in and out of life, Susan not you, you left a footprint in many people's hearts, my heart, a mark to last a lifetime and beyond. Your spirit, a spirit of grace, love and joy will live on through your wonderful parents Aunt Ann & Uncle John, incredible husband Kevin, beautiful daughters Molly, Nora, & Ella, such great brothers J.T. and Chris, and the many many people, family, and friends you touched with your grace throughout your life.

Thank you so much for the many lessons and awesome memories you shared and taught all of us, and all of the love you shared. You served the world so well with such class and dignity. You will be dearly missed, but know your spirit goes on, through all those you touched near and far, your heart goes on, and your ageless spunky smile & heart will always be forever young Susan!

♥♥♥♥♥♥♥♥♥♥♥♥♥♥♥♥♥♥♥♥♥♥♥♥♥♥♥♥♥♥♥♥♥♥♥♥

<u>Lucille St.Onge</u>

How I Remember Susan Dalton St.Onge

I felt like Susan was my second daughter. She arrived to me later in life. She was fully grown and helped fill a void in my life following the death of my beautiful daughter, Sandy, a year after Susan and Kevin were married. With her great beautiful smile and wonderful sense of humor, she became a necessary, valued and wonderful member of our family. When Kevin and Susan were married, I remember hearing Sandy say so happily that she "...finally has a sister"! She loved Susan and they would have been great friends.

Susan was loved by everyone in the Baillargeon and St.Onge families and we all enjoyed spending time with her. I believe she loved them too. I saw how empathetic Susan was when she and Kevin came to Berlin and many of us were at the St.Onge grandparents' home. We were all in different parts of the house while Pepere Edgar St.Onge was sitting alone in the living room in his favorite chair. Susan left a group to go sit with him to keep him company and to stop him from taking a nap!

I could not have asked for a better second daughter. I enjoyed the times we had together. Susan knew how to laugh and how to make others laugh. She loved to have fun and to play jokes on people and have jokes played on her.

Susan was quite an event planner! When Rich and I would get together with Susan and Kevin and their family, either in NJ or NH, she would plan outings for us to do together. We attended the Macy's Thanksgiving Day Parade. We spent another Thanksgiving in Gettysburg. We visited Williamsburg, Disney World and North Carolina. In New Hampshire, we took a train ride along Lake Winnipesaukee with the girls and went to many family parties. Times with her were always fun!

What I remember the most about Susan is the love she had for her family and for Kevin. She was an excellent mother to Molly, Nora and Ella. She would spend time and teach necessary skills and encourage them to laugh. She made sure they had everything they needed and encouraged them to participate in activities with other children. Even during the worst of her illness, when she was in the hospital, and asked for the girls to come for a visit, she took them to the candy machine to give them a treat. It was so important for her to spend that time with her girls as she was not able to be home with them.

Susan was a very generous person and mother. She allowed Rich and me to have the girls (one at a time) to spend time with us at our home. We enjoyed the one-on-one time and appreciated the opportunity to have a relationship with each and watch them grow up. I do have to boast that I helped with the potty training! They each spent time with me and all went home dry!

I am thankful that Susan left us a legacy of three beautiful daughters, three lovely young ladies. I have no doubt that in Heaven, she is watching over them and Kevin. She would be happy to know that they often talk about their Mom even though they miss her.

For sure, life would have been different for them (and for the rest of us) had Susan survived. Regrettably, that was not possible with her illness.

I have wonderful memories of her and lots of photos to remind me of how she came into this world and the impact she made. I am grateful that I was able to know her, that she married my son and became my friend.

May she Rest In Peace and spend time with her sister, Sandy, as she is missed by many people on earth.

♥♥

John Dalton

Recollections of a Father

Even as a young girl, Susan always was up for an adventure and unafraid of tackling the unknown. Here are my recollections of some of them.

Williamsburg, April 1979

Susan's older brothers were Boy Scouts and went on various camping trips during Spring Break. In 1979, their troop scheduled a canoe trip down the Shenandoah River. Coinciding with that trip, Ann and I decided to schedule our first trip to Colonial Williamsburg with Susan accompanying us.

We took the inland route through DC and, on arrival, spent a couple of days exploring the Governor's Palace, the Capitol and other sights. We had colonial-inspired pub fare for dinner at Chowning's Tavern; the second night we dined at the elegant Williamsburg Inn, with a harpist providing background music.

Given Susan's interest in all things equestrian, we decided to take the coastal route home, up the Delmarva peninsula via Route 50, past Assateague and Chincoteague Islands. Navigating the Chesapeake Bay Bridge-Tunnel was an interesting driving experience. Hours into the drive, as we reached Delaware, I asked Ann and Susan what the highlight of the trip was for them. In unison, they responded, "Dinner at the Williamsburg Inn."

If all they wanted was a nice dinner, I could have taken them to any one of a dozen excellent restaurants within a ten-mile radius of Westfield!

The Great Canoe Race, April 1981

Every year, the local Boy Scout Council sponsored a Great Canoe Race, 26 miles down the Delaware River, finishing at Bull's Island State Park, not far from Stockton (the small hotel

148

with the wishing well). The boys' troop participated every year, camping out on the Pennsylvania side of the river, staffing the lunch stop, and, of course, competing in the race.

I volunteered 12-year-old Susan and I to be one of the safety canoes, paddling behind the racers in the event anyone needed rescuing. It was a sunny, beautiful spring Saturday with near-perfect conditions for a leisurely trip down the Delaware River. And it was uneventful—no canoes swamped or needed rescuing—until we approached the finish line.

We had let our canoe drift to the left side of the river, forgetting that the finish line was just south of a coffer dam that had to be navigated through a flume that was in the middle of the river. With about 100 yards to go, I spotted the coffer dam, realized my error and called out to Susan, "Paddle left—HARD!"

We paddled furiously, barely making it to the flume with yards to spare and made it to the finish line. We were wet from breaking a sweat, but not from the embarrassment of being the safety canoe that almost swamped over the coffer dam!

Cheers – *Just A Few More Blocks, May 1983*

Susan's oldest brother was finishing his junior year at Boston University, and I was preparing to drive to Boston to bring him home after final exams. Ready for an adventure, Susan asked if she could accompany me on the journey. I explained that the car would be jam packed on the return trip and she would be stuck in the middle of the front seat (back then, sedans didn't have center consoles, just bench seats).

Susan agreed to the terms, and we drove to Boston on a beautiful spring day. We checked into the Howard Johnson's at Kenmore Square. We took the "T" downtown, wandered around Faneuil Hall, had dinner at Durgin Park and decided to head back to campus. Susan asked if we could see Cheers.

Premiering in 1982 and set in Boston, *Cheers* (where everybody knows your name) quickly became a top hit with a great cast. We agreed to ditch the "T" and walk to the bar's Beacon Hill location. Tired from the trip, Susan kept asking her brother how far it was. His repeated response, "It's just a few more blocks."

We reached Beacon Street and saw the bar. We were more than halfway back to the BU campus, so we continued walking up Boylston, stopped at Emack & Bolio's to have some ice cream for dessert, and finally reached our hotel. When we got to the room, Susan sprawled on her bed fully clothed and was asleep almost instantaneously.

The next morning, we had breakfast, checked out of the hotel, loaded-up the car. True to her word, Susan sat in the middle of the front seat and never once complained.

Macy's 4th Of July Fireworks, 1984

Susan and Grandma Dalton had a special relationship. Susan was a belated 60th birthday gift to Kay Dalton. Susan was born February 10, 1969; Kay Dalton was born February 9, 1909. She was thrilled to welcome the first Dalton girl after eleven consecutive Dalton boys.

They celebrated birthdays together, including Susan's Sweet Sixteen birthday dinner at the elegant Rainbow Room in Rockefeller Center. Grandma Dalton lived in Jersey City at the corner of Newark Avenue and Kennedy Boulevard, about a half-hour drive from Westfield. She had never learned to drive (my father tried to teach her, but, as he told it, we boys in the back seat objected). So, I routinely brought her to Westfield for family and holiday gatherings.

Grandma Dalton was with us for the 4th of July. When it was time for her to return home, Susan volunteered to accompany us.

We dropped Grandma Dalton off at her apartment as the sun was setting. Susan asked if there was some way that we could watch the Macy's fireworks over the Hudson River. I answered, "I think I know the perfect spot."

I drove to the foot of Pavonia Avenue, next to the long-abandoned Erie Railroad station. The area had already been cordoned off in anticipation of upcoming construction. I parked as close as I could get to the Hudson River and removed a flashlight from the glove box. We carefully made our way to the deteriorated ferry pier and had front-row seats for the spectacular Macy's 4th of July fireworks show. Other than the fireworks booms, the only noise we heard were the frightened rats skittering beneath the pier.

My First Employee (And Bill Collector) – 1987

I left the Deloitte partnership in late 1986 to start up my own consulting practice: Healthcare Business Specialists—assisting providers with the business aspects of healthcare delivery. Armed with contracts from Clara Maass Medical Center and Robert Wood Johnson University Hospital, I set up shop in shared office space in Cranford and started up the practice. We were successful in acquiring several hospital clients and hiring competent staff.

Susan was a senior at Westfield High School and became HBS's first employee, working part-time after school. She handled many of the administrative tasks. For example, as President-Elect of the New Jersey Chapter of the Healthcare Financial Management Association, one of my duties was to contract with the hotels where the monthly meetings would be held. Once the meeting calendar was set for the next year, Susan contacted the hotels and set up contracts (mostly at the Woodbridge Hilton) for the Chapter year.

151

Susan's duties also included following up with clients on past due bills. Given the nature of the practice, many of our largest clients were inner city safety net hospitals—notoriously slow payers. Making payroll was often a challenge. Often, our employees got paid in a timely manner, but the boss didn't. Fortunately, Ann was working, so my oft-delayed paycheck wasn't an issue.

Surprisingly, one of our slower-paying clients was Princeton Medical Center. On a Friday when we needed a client check to cover the next employee payroll, Susan called the Finance Department at Princeton to determine the status of the HBS bill for services. Their response: "We'll be mailing it out today." Always quick on her feet, Susan had heard "The check is in the mail" dodge before, so she said, "Just hold the check – I'm meeting a friend at the Quakerbridge Mall for dinner. I'll stop by on the way and pick it up."

Susan then drove to Princeton, picked up the check at the hospital, deposited it at the nearest branch of our bank, and payroll was covered.

♥♥♥♥♥♥♥♥♥♥♥♥♥♥♥♥♥♥♥♥♥♥♥♥♥♥♥♥♥♥♥♥♥♥♥♥♥♥♥

Ann Dalton

Recollections of a Mother

F. Scott Fitzgerald once wrote the following, "She was beautiful, but not like those girls in magazines. She was beautiful, for the way she thought. She was beautiful, for the sparkle in her eyes when she talked about something she loved. She was beautiful, for her ability to make other people smile, even if she was sad. No, she wasn't beautiful for something as temporary as her looks. She was beautiful, deep down to her soul. She is beautiful."

In my humble opinion, Fitzgerald could have been writing about Susan. She was a unique daughter. She was my daughter. She possessed many endearing qualities. Most importantly, she loved to be with people. She loved to enjoy other's company. She loved to share in their good times and be with them through their bad times. Susan enjoyed being "present" in as many ways as possible. She was present for the fun times at a party, just relaxing *at the beach, being with John and me and sharing herself with her own family, Kevin, Molly, Nora and Ella.*

    Personally, I cherish the times we spent together as mother and daughter. "My daughter Susan," I love how that sounds. She had such a sense of humor. I loved the subtleness with which she could get her point across. She was so diplomatic!

    I miss her. Losing her and missing her doesn't occupy every minute of the day as it used to but, I feel her presence and I know that she is with me and all her family and extended family and friends. Several times since she left us I have felt her Spirit. I have felt her Spirit in the birds who sing to me, the Monarch butterflies who come closer than typical. Because of this, I feel that she is in a good place and happy.

    A few years ago, I thought that I had lost my wedding ring. I searched everywhere, but never mentioned it to John. It must have been "gone" for a year or more. That time period included a physical move from our primary residence in Edison to

Manasquan after Tropical Storm Ida flooded our condo. Thinking my ring was gone for good, I was resigned to that fact. Then, we were staying at a Hampton Inn in New Hampshire visiting Kevin and the girls. Getting into bed, I took my slippers off and saw something embedded in the sole of my slipper. I looked down and – OMG!!! John was sound asleep, I didn't wake him, but there it was, my wedding ring! I believe Susan was watching out for me! Thank you Susan!

Last year, we received flowers from Susan's BFF/maid of honor/little sister Susan Howell on June 21 marking the date my Susan passed. It was a gorgeous floral arrangement from "little Sue." A couple of hours later, another gorgeous floral arrangement arrived from little Sue (see photo). Little Sue had only ordered one arrangement but we got two! Side by side, big Sue and little Sue! I believe my daughter Susan had a hand in that!

We love you Susan, and miss you every day. Your love is with us through your wonderful and loving daughters, Molly, Nora and Ella. They are becoming their own independent women, like you were, and yet even with that, we see your attributes in them! They miss you, they love you and they think of you often as they strive to make you proud.

♥♥♥♥♥♥♥♥♥♥♥♥♥♥♥♥♥♥♥♥♥♥♥♥♥♥♥♥♥♥♥♥

Cousin Rebecca Shafer DeJesus

The Last Night

It was a tragic comedy of errors that resulted in me spending the night with Susan and Kevin at the hospice center. Miscommunication, inferred sentiments, and deferred honesty tended to be the norm in our family. Nevertheless, there I was.

I waited in the common area with my Mom to enter Susan's room. Where we did, the first thing I noticed was the peace that pervaded the space. The lights were dimmed just enough so that the rays of the late afternoon sun peeking in through the window illuminated her porcelain, silky skin. The silence that surrounded us was one of those kinds that at once made you feel uncomfortable, nervous, and unsteady on your feet. However, at the same time, it was the type of silence that tempted you to say everything you've ever wanted to say but always held back. When I first tried to speak, I stumbled over my sentences. Then, firm in my resolve, I let down my guard. I looked Susan right in the eyes and said, "I love you. I love you so much."

Subdued by the medicine and quieted by the cancer that was taking her, she slightly turned her chin towards me, and a few tears fell from her eyes. She wasn't able to speak. I grabbed her hand and squeezed it hard.

Back in the common area, more people were filtering in and out. We traded stories, food, consolation, and strength. There was a shared, pervasive sense of toeing the line between saying too much and being reserved and overly polite.

As the evening wore on, and the remaining few milled about, I grew increasingly concerned about my own mother. Earlier, I noticed more than ever how she and Susan shared the same stunning cheekbones, wide-open smile, and sky-blue eyes. Mom had driven up from Ocean County, and it was now well beyond

9pm. I frantically searched for local hotels as I was worried about Mom driving the Garden State Parkway South such a long distance at what would be such a late hour of night. No luck. Reluctantly I kissed her goodbye and made her promise to confirm her return home safe and sound. Staying with Aunt Ann and Uncle John was not possible for some reason. Knowing that, at best, Susan might make it through until tomorrow afternoon, I was torn. I had left vacation early, taking four different flights and traveling a total of about 18 hours to be here with her. Exhaustion was creeping down my spine.

Kevin graciously offered that I could stay there with them, for what would be The Last Night. I am forever grateful to him, even though at the time I felt like a felonious third wheel, stealing the last bits of forever that he was able to spend with his beloved.

The Last Phone Call with Susan was just a couple weeks prior. It all happened so fast, yet somehow time also seemed to slow way down. I can't tell you exactly how many minutes passed, but the next few hours simultaneously went by in the blink of an eye while they dragged on forever.

For the bulk of what my grievous memory serves, Kevin and I were on alternate sides of the bed. He on Susan's right, clasping her feeble hand with both of his, and me on her left doing the same. Neither one of us wanted to sleep lest we miss the last few precious moments that we could steal from Father Time. With any slight hint that life might be exiting her, I jolted upright, scanning her eyes and lips for any sign of movement. The few times that I dozed off I immediately woke, my eyes darting towards her belly and ribs to see if, in the dawning hours of the night, I could still hear the rattly up-down-in-out groans of her fading breath.

At one point I noticed Kevin falling asleep. I so very much wanted to wake him and sometimes still regret that I didn't. But at the same time, I knew how utterly exhausted he already was,

157

and how much strength he would need in the days to come. I had also heard and read many stories of death, and how sometimes the dying will wait until their lover leaves. I can't pretend to know what the reality was. But knowing how deeply and fully Susan loved Kevin, I strongly believe what she wanted most, more than anything else, was for him to take the rest that he so very much needed.

When her last breath finally arrived, I was taken aback by its innocence and lack of fanfare. I guess I envisioned some type of final heave, a concluding hymn for a body that had fought so hard for so long. Then again, just like her life, Susan's death was proud and ethereal. So as I sat there for a few moments, I vacillated between finding a nurse, waking Kevin, and just letting her be.

I had only been in The Hospice Center for less than 12 hours, but given its size, I was amazed how long it took me to find someone. I was hallucinating from lack of sleep, and it felt otherworldly. I kept finding abandoned desks; bumping into dead-end hallways; and opening doors to empty rooms. There was a high-pitched, buzzing hum all throughout that drowned my sense of space and time. When I returned to the room, nurse in tow, we found Kevin slumped over her. Years of love, regret, yearning, and joy teemed from his body. I can't ever know what he lost in that moment, but I know it was grand. Decades of being by someone's side; raising children together; surfing life's lows and highs.

The remaining time was spent making phone calls, waking people from their sleep with the most-dreaded news. Quickly shifting into get-things-done mode, Kevin expertly navigated his new unknown wilderness. I tried my best to just be a person in the room, a warm body to help him get things done. It was hard to cast my sadness to the side, but I wanted to be there for him, the way that Susan was always there for me. I agreed to go with him to help break the news to their three young daughters. I'm still glad that there was a few hours until we could wake them and break the news. In those few hours I sat across from Kevin at the diner, both of us staring into our bacon, egg, and cheese sandwiches, trembling from hunger but too devastated to eat. I spent that time praying for courage because I had to help break the hearts of three incredibly sweet girls who were simply lovesick for their Mom that was never coming home.

The awkwardness of having been there with Kevin when Susan died has faded, although it hasn't fully gone away. In part, it felt intrusive, like spying on someone during a sacred and holy private moment. But mostly, I've accepted that, for whatever reason, I was meant to be there. In some ways, it's a blip on the timeline of my 47-year-old life. But mostly, it's an experience that I'll cherish forever: bearing witness to someone I love lifting the veil and passing through. And being able to be there to hold tightly the ones she left behind.

♥♥♥♥♥♥♥♥♥♥♥♥♥♥♥♥♥♥♥♥♥♥♥♥♥♥♥♥♥♥♥♥♥♥♥

Chapter 17
Susan Thinks Ahead

Susan wrote three email "letters" anticipating her death. One was to her daughters. One was to her "Mom Crew." One was to me.

Almost six years after Susan passed, I was cleaning up some files on the family hard drive and I came across one simply titled "SDSO.doc". It was in her folder but I had not previously seen it or made note of it. It was a typewritten letter to her girls. I am not exactly sure when she wrote it but the date and time stamp on the file is June 5, 2017, a little over one year before she passed. I don't believe she ever sent or gave it to them. If she did, she never told me and they had no recollection of it. I did share it with them while writing this book.

The email to her girls shows the depth of her maternal instincts and more importantly just how much she loved them. Fiercely. And, she told them she loved ME and that I was handsome. She gave them great practical advice. I wish I could include it here but Susan wrote it for her girls.

♥♥♥♥♥♥♥♥♥♥♥♥♥♥♥♥♥♥♥♥♥♥♥♥♥♥♥♥♥♥♥♥♥♥♥♥♥♥♥

I have no idea whether she ever circulated the email she drafted to her Mom Crew. I don't think she did. I found it about a month after she passed. Like the one to our girls, she appears to have written it about a year before she passed.

The Mom Crew consists of women she hoped would continue to watch over her girls. Her message to them reads as a "How To" care instruction for Molly, Nora and Ella as only a Mother could write.

The Crew

My "Mom" Crew,

I am looking to you for help and guidance.

You have been an amazing friend to me for many years. There are so many wonderful qualities about you that I respect and admire and wish for you to instill those qualities into my girls. It's going to take a Village – I'm so proud that you are part of my Village.

This is a big request, but one I know I can entrust to you. Molly, Nora and Ella are Mommy's girls. I am so proud to be a mom, especially theirs, and I made it my mission to have a strong bond with them. My girls love to snuggle, hug and kiss. (Play games, sit and read with them; Movie nights are a plus.)

Please show my girls that life is beautiful despite bad things. Make them smile - they light up from within -- I do not want them to lose their inner light/confidence/self-esteem/self-worth/beauty. Please let them know that they are loved, always, and should be free to express themselves. All three are very sensitive and handle things differently. Please encourage them to open up to you and express themselves. I always told them to speak respectfully (not be bitchy or act entitled -- not that it always works!) since I want them to have manners and behave accordingly. Also, I want to encourage a strong sisterly bond so they will always have each other.

Trust is huge in our family. We have an open communication policy about anything going on in their lives. I always told my girls that they could ask me anything -- even if it meant they would get into trouble or it was uncomfortable -- I wanted them to know that my job is to help and guide them and that I am always here for them. Good or bad. I want them to know that I

161

trust and believe in them. Empower them. Please help them when they're feeling lost. I always welcome their inquiries and try to NEVER come from a place of no -- I don't want to lose their trust. If we disagree, we discuss options and solutions. Give them choices. Text them. Call them. Let them know you're there. They're going to need female advice. I need you to be the ears on the ground. (BTW -- no dating until Senior year of HS and family must approve.)

And, Kevin. This is going to be hardest on him. Yes, he is tightly wound but a very loving, caring, witty, family-oriented and smart guy who treats women with respect. I know he's going to need help and a tremendous amount of patience. I want my girls to look up to their father and love him (which they do). I don't know how to best say this, but, I believe you'll be the best support system for him. Please share whatever necessary with him -- I cannot stress it enough how much he's going to need your guidance and I know he will be extremely appreciative of your input.

Also, I have asked him not to date until the girls are much older and have the emotional maturity to handle such a change. I do not want him to re-marry. That would break my heart.

Also, this is big -- shopping, hair cuts, hygiene products, girly stuff, birds and bees, girl drama, etc. They're going to need clothes, etc., and I believe you all know my style/taste (as well as letting them explore their own style -- no ghetto/hoochie/cheap). This is an area that I know Kevin will absolutely need help. Please take them shopping, mani/pedi's, haircuts and make it fun for them. Bring them to your home, or, kick Kevin out one night and spend the day/evening here with them. I know he is absolutely going to need help with grocery shopping and meals (esp. w/Ella's allergies). He makes a mean bowl of Cheerio's.

Molly -- big-hearted, always kind, creative, silly/goofy, loves horseback riding and marching band, loves to read, has ADHD (inattentive, operates slowly) and has a 504 in school. I'll tease her that she'll sometimes (mentally) wander off the reservation.

Nora -- a worrier (can get anxious), silly/goofy, extremely conscientious and always thinking of others, loves to sing and theater, creative, loves bike riding, has ADHD (impulsive, hyper) and IEP in school. We would tease that her nickname should be "Norus-interruptus".

Ella -- big talker, silly/goofy, loves minecraft and playing games, loves to read, has Tree Nut and Sesame allergy -- MUST carry EpiPens at all times. Also, carry Tums. She has Acid Reflux and it acts up when she's anxious or stressed. I have a binder with all her medical info and how to distinguish between Food Allergy reaction and Acid Reflux. Going to a Restaurant you MUST speak directly to the Manager or the Chef and tell them her allergies (sometimes, call ahead). They'll work with you. If they won't, find another restaurant. (Pam and Ann -- you're the best resource to help Kevin understanding her allergies and managing them.)

Also, the big stuff. The Milestones. Dances, proms, graduations, college, dating, careers, wedding and having their own families. I can't express it enough. Be there for them, and for me.

Please encourage them to talk about me and all our fun memories. Look at pictures and videos. Talk about things we've done together as well. Please let them know that I will always be proud of them. I will always be their Mom and my love for them is infinite.

Sue Letwink	Annalisa Dalton
Alisa Wasserman	Denise Ferbas
Amy Hosmer	Rebecca DeJesus
Annemarie Augenstein	Lori Fitzgerald

Terrine Joe	*Colleen O'Hearn*
Jen Glander	*Barbara Vanderhayden*
Alexis Calabrese	*Melia Gorsak*
Pam Magee	*Tracey Ingersoll*
Jessica Cerrino	*Jane St.Onge*
Sharee Carrow	*Becky St.Onge*
Lisa Taylor	*Betty St.Onge*
Kathy Maloney	*Kathy Berthiaume*
Emma Maloney	*Holly Friedman*

♥♥♥♥♥♥♥♥♥♥♥♥♥♥♥♥♥♥♥♥♥♥♥♥♥♥♥♥♥♥♥♥♥♥♥♥

Sent or not, this letter, like her message to her daughters, speaks for itself.

Likewise, her unsent email to me is incredibly heart-felt. I found it in her account on July 3, 2018. Candidly, there are some things set-forth in it that were, and continue to be, hard for me to read. With time and perspective, however, I have come to terms that these are the words of a strong, independent and loving woman who was enduring incredible stress, facing her mortality and losing her family.

As difficult as it is, I include her letter to me here for anyone who may derive strength, guidance and/or solace in her words.

5/19/17

Kevin

You are an incredible, loving, husband and father. You are my rock. You're smart, funny, handsome and are able to make sure things get done. Please don't forget that. Yes, you blow up and have your moments. But, keep it in check and make sure you apologize to the girls and model good behavior for them. I want them to see you as a role model for their future husbands. At times things will be overwhelming. You need to give yourself a break and relax. Take a deep breath and step back. I will forever be with you, everyday.

I envisioned us together, growing old, raising our daughters, celebrating special moments and events, wedding dress shopping, becoming grandparents, traveling and rubbing arthritis cream on each other. You and our girls have been the most precious and rewarding part of my life. Treasure them, and all our time together. Please make sure that our girls are taken care of physically, financially and emotionally.

These are our girls that you are raising. I take pride in our family and how we have raised them. Please make sure you tell them and show them they are loved, everyday. They are your priority. However, give yourself time and be forgiving. Ask some of my "mom crew" friends and family to come spend time with them (ie, on a weekend) so you can have time for yourself. Make sure they are surrounded by people who share our same ideals and values.

Talk to them. Ask them about their day. Let them open up to you and share their feelings. You and your daughters are very similar in that you like to talk and share your day, conversations and observations. Sure, it may not be the exciting topics you may want to hear about, but, your influence and being present is important. Empower them. Show them that life is an adventure and to embrace it.

Make sure you know their friends. Check their text messages, social media. Have their friends hang out here so you can see and hear what is going on. So what if they make a mess -- that's easier to clean up than unnecessary drama or other "events" or incidents that can go seriously wrong.

Let them find their passion and support them. Again, it may not be what excites you, but it's going to show support, instill drive and motivation in them. Make sure they go to a college close (within 2 hours) to home -- you'll want them close by. They are going to take care of you as well.

There are going to be difficult days. Please don't let them overwhelm you. Let your parents, my parents, family and friends help. Please remind our parents to not judge the girls, belittle them, and be passive aggressive. That'll only shut them off to communicating and lead the girls to not trust them.

You're going to need female support and advice. Ask for help (Susan, Amy, Rebecca, Alisa, Denise, Annalisa, Tracy Ingersoll, Jane St.Onge, Kathy Berthiaume). You're going to need their guidance on topics that will be beyond your realm.

Clothing shopping, medical questions, haircuts, Christmas and birthday gifts, please let their God-mothers help you and encourage our girls to have relationships with each of them. Don't let the girls clam up and make sure they call their aunts, our friends, family, your cousins, whomever they feel comfortable speaking to.

I know you're going to be lonely and you'll need to talk to people, and make sure you (all) go to therapy.

This is something I feel quite strongly about -- please do not date until the girls are older and have the emotional maturity to handle such a change. They are going to be very protective of you and will be jealous. I do not want you re-marry. That would break my heart. I signed up to spend my life with you here and ever after.

I have written birthday cards for them. Please give them a card each year.

I have come to embrace (not necessarily agree with) everything in her message and it simply makes me love her all the more.

Chapter 18
How Do I Say Goodbye?

June 30, 2018
St. Helen's Church
Westfield, New Jersey

In that moment, as the Celebration of Life was concluding, I was awash in thought, "How do I conclude these remembrance remarks, these amazing stories, when I simply wanted to stay in the moment with all-things-Susan?"

From the podium again (did I mention that I love a good podium and microphone?), I forged ahead.

With those and countless other stories in mind, I wanted to share two final writings. The first is a poem I wrote on our 20th Wedding Anniversary, one of her first days of chemotherapy:

October 1, 2014

> *20 years ago today I said "I do"*
>
> *Lucky for me, Susan said she did too - phew!*
>
> *And so it goes, laughter, tears*
>
> *Warm hugs, cold beers*
>
> *Friends, family, children, joy*
>
> *Life's challenges - oh boy...*
>
> *We will spend today getting her well*
>
> *Cancer, stupid cancer, has cast its spell*
>
> *Slow us down for awhile, it may*
>
> *But today, tomorrow, forever, I will say*
>
> *I am so glad I said "I do"*
>
> *Even more so that she said she did too...*

In conclusion I want to share a letter I wrote to Susan the day after she passed. Molly, Nora, Ella and I arranged an ensemble of her clothing and other mementos to have cremated with her. Included were letters Molly, Nora and I wrote to her. Nora suggested that a new family tradition will be to write Mommy letters on June 21ˢᵗ each year telling her all about our lives over the past year and then burning them in our fire pit while we roast marshmallows.

Here is my letter.

June 22, 2018

Dear Susan,

On our wedding day, when we recited our vows, including the words "...til death do us part..." I never imagined this. I never imagined standing here alone, celebrating your life, but feeling, indeed <u>being</u>, utterly alone in this world for the first time in 27 years.

Parted.

I never imagined NOT growing old with you.

Your presence in my life, your love for me, our time together, our children – it was all a gift from God.

All the years together, all the growth, challenges, failures, triumphs, joy – our journey was simply incredible. You made me a better person and for that I will always be grateful.

From the very first day we met, I longed to be near you. The distance years during law school were torture. Our few weekends together were bliss. I knew early on that I wanted to marry you and be with you forever!

For over two decades, every time we were apart I knew I would see you again. And, even if we were only apart for a few minutes, I might have only been one room away, but when I would see you again, my heart beat differently. It beat fully and completely. Your energy, your high vibrations, carried me and inspired me.

I can't believe you are gone.

I believed you when you said you would beat cancer.

I am so sorry I was so naive.

I am so sorry I couldn't be stronger for you and have seen through the coded conversations you had with Dr. Wax.

Two days ago, our foreheads touching as you stubbornly clung to life, I did the hardest thing I ever had to do – the hardest thing I hope to never have to do again.

I told you it was ok to go.

I told you that I don't blame God for wanting you in Heaven. If I were Him, I would want you there too, with me, forever.

I told you I would take care of our girls, and I will.

I reminded you of my first words to you. I want to believe that you heard me that night, your final night in this realm.

I want to believe that you heard me say that from the beginning you were the one, you were always the one.

I love you Susan.

I will always love you.

You are the one.

You will always be the one.

Your loving husband,

Kevin

Xoxoxo

In celebration and memory of

Susan Dalton St. Onge

February 10, 1969 ~ June 21, 2018

Devoted Daughter
Caring Sister
Loyal Friend
Loving Wife
Adoring Mother

A DRINKING SONG

Wine comes in at the mouth And love
comes in at the eye; That's all we shall
know for truth Before we grow old and
die. I lift the glass to my mouth, I look
at you, and sigh.

— W.B. Yeats

Facebook Post

June 21, 2021

Today at 3:00 AM marked three years since cancer took our Susan.

Not a day goes by that she isn't thought of with love.

My grief and healing, stunted for a long time by questionable decisions and a refusal to acknowledge reality, has morphed into stubborn acceptance. Even so, it has taken me a long time to be able to look at pictures and videos of our life together. Recently, however, I re-watched her 40th Birthday Video and it changed things for me.

I hope Facebook doesn't take the audio track off because I am re-posting the video.

As difficult as it is, I know that life here goes on for the rest of us. As such, Molly, Nora, Ella and I deserve to know the joy in this lifetime that Susan knew in hers. That video reminded me of her joy - and that I was a privileged part of it for 27 years, as were many of you...

So, today, I resolve with you, my Facebook Friends and Family, to choose to be inspired by the life that Susan lived and be the smile that she was for so many people. Be the laughter that she caused for so many. Be the warmth and comfort that she was, and continues to be, for so many.

Tears will still come but with your help, and hers, I want to open my heart to happiness, the way she did. Open my heart to love, the way she did.

As you may know, she taught me that love is an acronym:

L et

O thers

V ibrate

E qually

Because her love, her vibrations, were so strong, I believe it is our turn, my turn, to elevate my own vibrations in her honor.

We miss you Susan.

We love you Susan.

I love you Susan.

I always will…

You reduce me to love …

Susan's Charities

Before she passed, during her final days, Susan requested that donations in lieu of flowers may be made in her memory to the Wilkes University Women's Soccer Team and/or The Pembroke Welsh Corgi Club of the Garden State. Anyone reading this book who may be inclined, may still make donations in her name as follows:

Wilkes University
Office of Advancement & Alumni Engagement
Attention: Gifts Officer
84 West South Street
Wilkes Barre, PA 18766
1-800-WILKES-U

www.wilkes.edu

 Please note gift for "Women's Soccer Team on behalf of Susan Dalton St.Onge

In addition to The Pembroke Welsh Corgi Club of the Garden State, there are two other Corgi-based organizations to which donations may be made in Susan's name.

– The Pembroke Welsh Corgi Club of the Garden State

www.pwccgs.org

– Mayflower Pembroke Welsh Corgi Club (covers the New England states)

www.mayflowercorgiclub.org

– Pembroke Welsh Corgi Club of the Potomac (covers the mid-Atlantic states)

www.pwccp.org

Please note gift made on behalf of Susan Dalton St.Onge

Special thanks for their contributions to this book, and/or for their special friendship and support through these many years, go to the following (if I omitted anyone who should be included, it is entirely my fault and I apologize):

John and Ann Dalton

Lucille and Richard St.Onge

Tom Hanna

Susan Letwink Howell

Rebecca DeJesus Shafer

Matthew Shafer

Amanda and Terry Hosmer

Alisa Tagliareni Wasserman

Laura McCord Donnelly

Tracey Ryan McCarrick

Birgit Berkow

Emily Berkow

Uncle Ron St.Onge

Aunt Jackie St.Onge

Christine Chaillet

Dina Gavenas

Steve Hoffmann

Joanne Prokopowicz Sears

Nicholas Tremblay

Meg B.

Stephan Kolodiy

Mark Sapara

Jennifer Russell Yearwood

Kathy Carsillo

Melissa Carsillo

Sue Sabol

Karen Tebbin-Rossi

Mike and Lisa Taylor

Kerriann Broussard

Sue Sabol

Jerry Rickrode

Dr. Maggie Tieman, PsyD

Carol Hicks White, Grief Counselor, Center for Hope Hospice and Palliative Care, Scotch Plains, NJ

Father Michael Saporito, St. Helen's Parish, Westfield, NJ

Overlook Hospital, Summit, NJ

Author's Note

I would be remiss not to mention that Susan has two brothers and sisters-in-law, together with a niece and a nephew. The brothers and sisters-in-law were kept informed of Susan's declining health during her final days and were specifically included in family meetings at the hospital with the doctors. They also visited Susan at the hospital and in Hospice.

For reasons known only to them, they have chosen to largely absent themselves from her families' lives since her passing. Hurt people hurt people and my girls and I were definitely hurting in the years following Susan's death. I am sure they were too.

I have limited most references (with a few notable exceptions) to their roles in Susan's life in this book out of respect for their chosen privacy. I love them and miss them but will respect their absence and hope that someday they may be willing to reconcile, in some way. I wish them well and hold out hope.

Epilogue I

Susan shared her wishes with me during her final days. She did not want a formal Funeral Mass but a Celebration of Life. That turned out to be harder than one would think as I had to argue with an extremely conservative associate pastor from South America at St. Helen's Parish to allow it in the Church.

Then Pastor, Father Michael Saporito, mediated the apparent "issue" and facilitated Susan's wishes, but that experience did more to turn me off to organized religion than most anything else in my life. Don't get me wrong, I believe in God and his Son, Jesus Christ. I am learning to read and understand the Bible, now, more than ever, but I now believe that structured religion is not Faith.

Again, I digress.

Susan requested to be cremated. She also requested a keg at the luncheon following her Celebration of Life. I completely forgot about the keg. She has reminded me, in her own way, since…

She requested four urns: one primary urn for me and three smaller ones, one for each of her daughters. She requested that I arrange to have our ashes commingled and scattered off the jetty in Manasquan, New Jersey, and in Lake Winnipesaukee, New Hampshire.

I selected an urn set with etched butterflies in a garden done in light pink hues. I have been told by those who knew Susan best that they completely and totally capture her essence. I hope so. I'm so sorry I forgot the keg.

Epilogue II

Susan has given me many gifts.

Her love.
Our children.
Great meals.
Laughs.
Tears.
The list goes on.

Two gifts, however, stand out to me as most significant.

She gave herself to me for 27 years. I will always be honored by her conscious decision to choose to be with me. It is a memory I will always treasure.

She has also given me the opportunity to experience a second love of a lifetime.

Consistent with Letting Others Vibrate Equally (L-O-V-E), with her spiritual guidance, I will give and receive love again.

I know I will.

I know she will make sure of it.

About the Author

Susan and Kevin
Dublin, Ireland
2011

In addition to being Susan's widower and father to their three daughters, Kevin M. St.Onge is an NCAAW division two and three basketball referee. He also works boys and girls high school varsity games and teaches new officials. He is trained as a lawyer and has reinvented himself, professionally, several times. His passions, however, beyond his children, are rooted in sports, media and finding the most efficient way to mow his lawn. He serves as the voice of Milford Spartan Football (his old high school team) on local access television but is rarely seen on-air, having a self-described "face made for radio." He loves Broadway shows but could do without all the singing and dancing. Returning to Milford, New Hampshire, following Susan's passing, Kevin is just trying to be a nice guy and provide for his family. Some days he's better at it than others.

www.ingramcontent.com/pod-product-compliance
Lightning Source LLC
Chambersburg PA
CBHW051156120626
46547CB00012B/1081